Adolf Hitler

Pictures from the Life of the Führer

1931–1935

Adolf Hitler

Pictures from the Life of the Führer
1931–1935

ENCOMIUM: Hermann Göring

FOREWORD: Joseph Goebbels

TEXT: Joseph Goebbels, Robert Ley, Albert Speer,
Baldur von Schirach, Fritz Todt, Otto Dietrich, and others

TRANSLATED FROM THE 1936 EDITION:

Carl Underhill Quinn

INTRODUCTION AND COMMENTARY:

Rabbi Julius Rosenthal, PH.D., D.D., M.H.L.

PEEBLES PRESS

NEW YORK / LONDON

First published 1978 by
Peebles Press International, Inc.
10 Columbus Circle, New York, New York 10019

© 1978 Peebles Press International, Inc.
ISBN 0-85690-065-6
Library of Congress Catalog Card Number 77-20715

Distributed by
The Bobbs-Merrill Co., Inc.
4300 West 62nd St.
Indianapolis, Indiana 46268, U.S.A.
in the United States and Canada

Barrie & Jenkins
24 Highbury Crescent
London N5 1RX, England
in the U.K., Ireland, Australia, New Zealand and South Africa

DESIGNED BY JACQUES CHAZAUD

Printed and bound in the United States of America

cc

Contents

Introduction

hy deal with Hitler again? Why translate this arch-Nazi document, a collection of essays by high officials, each describing the genius of the Chief?

The renewed wave of interest in the meaning of Nazism, which goes by the name *die Hitlerwelle* in Germany and is mounting all over the world, has produced enough writings to fill a small library. At the very outset, I wish to emphasize that this book is different from most of the others. They often represent careful, scholarly investigation, very valuable, of course. ADOLF HITLER is the raw material of history, intended in this edition not primarily to be tested for truth or falsehood of content—it is obviously full of lies and distortions—but to be quarried for a true conception of how the Nazis wished to perceive themselves and to be perceived by the German nation.

The neo-Nazis might try to exploit this document. "Ah, you say Hitler was a monster? Don't you realize you are succumbing to Jewish lies? Judge Wilhelm Staeglich has already proved that the ovens of Auschwitz were really bakeries (*Nation Europa*, Oct., 1973). Arthur R. Butz, Associate Professor of Electrical Engineering at Northwestern University, has demonstrated that nowhere near six million Jews perished in the concentration camps; it was only three million and they, not by design, but by unavoidable wartime hunger and disease. (*The New York Times*, Dec. 28, 1976) Now, look at this book, ADOLF HITLER. See what a genius he was and how beloved of the German people!"

Adolf Hitler aspired to build a thousand-year Aryan Empire and to live on in history forever. This book brings additional attention to him and might even add to the fulfillment of the first dream, the Empire, considering the impossibility of permanently dividing Germany given the prodigious capacities of its inhabitants and its supremely strategic location.

This book is being published with faith in human intelligence and decency. Anyone prepared to believe its contents and not be sickened by every statement and claim is terribly misguided. Professor Butz is crazy or wicked or both and probably beyond redemption with or without the book. But those who now repudiate him and all his works in historical hindsight still require material such as is in this publication in order to grasp the reason for his hold on his people.

I think of the case of Albert Speer. His two books from prison seem to be sincere repentance. Nevertheless, I have some questions. He represents himself as a misled technician: I doubt that any man of his status could have been all that innocent of the atrocities. He even sneers at Hitler's architectural ability. "His real preferences were for arched passageways, domes, curving lines, ostentation, always with an element of elegance—in short, the baroque . . . I observed that he did not know how to convey in his sketches the ornateness he extolled in words." (SPANDAU, New York, 1977)

These questions are sharpened when we read in this translation the young, enthusiastic Albert Speer. ". . . The Führer started out . . . with singular experience as a master-builder. He created stone buildings which are sure to give evidence of a cultural capability for making something that will cause the people's age of greatness to last a thousand years." And, "For him art is his highest objective." Was he dissembling then—or now?

Without additional information one has to proceed on the basis of impressions. It is my impression that he was sincere then and is sincere now. I believe he was swept along in a crashing wave of enthusiasm which embraced not only politics but the whole idea of Germany revived by touching the earth of restored traditional values in all of culture, including art and architecture. Now it has all turned to ashes in his mouth.

In my opinion, the marriage of the Führer and his nation is the most important matter to be illuminated by this book. We are tempted, and I am sure Germans are more strongly tempted, to imagine good people supporting the Movement with a pistol at their heads. Brutal coercion by all means suffused the system and suppressed some opposition but a great nation is not a gentle suburban home taken over by gun-wielding escaped convicts. Since the lesson of the 1923 Putsch, the National Socialist Party sought to appropriate State power by legitimate means facilitated by strong-arm methods where feasible. It was primarily by legitimate means that it finally came to power. On August 19, 1934, some 95 percent of the registered German voters went to the polls and 90 percent, more than 38 million of them, voted Hitler total governmental power. On March 7, 1936, some 99 percent of the 45,453,691 registered voters passed on the annexation of the Rhineland and 98.8 percent approved. Granted, no election anywhere ever precisely measures the sentiment of the voters, though we can hope that in the United States we do not emulate the tactics of the Kochem S.D. in marking the ballots with skim milk; then beating up the nay-sayers. But having carefully studied the results of several German elections and referendums down to the electoral district level, I am prepared to declare that they do not deviate from a projection of the normal accretion plus near-zero and minus 9 to 13 percent. In other words, the vast majority of the German people stood behind Hitler.

So do not denigrate Otto Dietrich when he claims, "Nowhere in the world is there such a fanatical love on the part of millions for one man . . . it grows slowly and impressively. It does not appear with some furious impetuosity on one single occasion. It is always there, at every moment and with every German." Do not say: What would you expect from the Press Chief of the Party and later, of the State? As the Leader saw it, as this follower saw it and as the majority of the German people saw it, opponents constituted an unwanted nation of Marxists and Jews; the true nation was for Hitler or *was* Hitler and he, Germany. "Christ has come to us through Adolf Hitler," crooned a Thuringian churchwarden in 1936 and the Führer himself was prepared to enlist God into his activities. "Lord, You see, we have changed; the German nation is no longer the nation of dishonor, of shame, of self-laceration, of timidity and little faith; no, Lord, the German nation has once more grown strong in spirit, strong in will, strong in persistence, strong in enduring all sacrifices. Lord, we will not swerve from You; now bless our struggle." (Address of May 1, 1933, Berlin. Joachim Fest, HITLER, New York, 1973)

And what *would* you expect from the Nazi Press Director and his colleagues? I have already indicated: considerable sincerity, for one, or sincere self-deception, if you prefer. These men had pledged their total beings to the cause. It is impossible to maintain such a commitment absolutely cynically. You would also expect propaganda. It has been said that the Nazis drove the German people crazy with their propaganda. Let us consider the question: did the Nazis drive others mad or were they themselves crazy? The notion that the Nazis were insane is advocated by many students of mental illness.

They see the Movement as being a gang of individuals with pathologically slippery holds on reality, perverted and distorted, seizing control of a powerful country and translating the vapors of their sick minds into national ruin. To diagnose Hitler, they say, you must use the same tools as for Charles Manson (who is much occupied with the German leader) and for Jake Dunsmore (who is supposed to have persuaded officials of a State penitentiary to release him into the Army in World War II and then swiftly proceeded to slit his training sergeant's throat).

The theory satisfies some of our own needs. We need to deny any hint that we ourselves might act like Nazis. People act that way only if they are maternally deprived or their body chemistry is unbalanced or they are brain-damaged; not people who are reasonably sound of mind, limb, brain and upbringing. We need to be reassured that there is a way of preventing such a disaster in the future and if the problem is mental illness, then a safeguard is at hand: psychiatric screening of candidates for high office. The techniques which might have rejected Senator Eagleton and President Nixon might also have detected the underlying hysteria of many Nazi leaders. Placing it all on the level of emotional pathology also airs out malodorous guilt. It absolves the British for bestowing the gift of a navy on a "peace-loving" Germany; it absolves the French for sticking to the Maginot Line instead of stopping Hitler in the Rhineland because they believed a sane tactician would go no further; it absolves Jews who were certain that no German executive could wish to persecute real German Jews—it was the Polish Jews he was after and that was reasonable; it absolves the millions of followers, unaware that a madman had the reins in his hands; yes, it absolves the Nazis themselves. They were not bad; only sick.

I am not impressed. Firstly, as to the good Germans, a Jewish cattle-dealer from Swabia told me of the day he fled the village where his family had lived for four hundred years. As he, with his wife and daughters, walked toward the railroad station, not a single person came out to say goodbye; every house was shut tight; every blind was drawn—except for a tiny gap for the watching eyes.

Then, who shall be impaneled for our imaginary psychiatric screening committee? Would you, in 1933, have accepted the nomination of C.G. Jung, a towering genius in the field? That was the year he obliged the Nazis by becoming President of the professional psychoanalytic association and Editor of its journal, *Zentralblatt für Psychotherapie,* under such conditions of membership as exclusion of Jews and each affiliate being required to read MEIN KAMPF. In 1936 he was joined by a co-editor named Hermann Göring. (Ernest Jones, THE LIFE AND WORKS OF SIGMUND FREUD, New York, 1957) Since normality is in any case a statistical concept, I suppose one would have to say that it was Jung and the peekers-behind-the-blinds who were sane and the opponents of Hitler, crazy.

Nor do I believe the Nazis can be considered lunatics. Madmen do not lead nations. From my own experience as chaplain in two of the largest mental hospitals in the State of New York as well as in a progressive residential treatment center for disturbed adolescents, which does not render me an expert in the field but does enable me to draw some conclusions, I would say that nothing would frighten an insane person more than the power to actualize fantasies. His ego participates in the process of cognition only within its sealed sphere and not upon encountering reality. There is no flexibility, no consistency, no sustained mobilization of psychic and material resources toward a defined goal. We have but to consider the serpentine political elegance of the Nazi rise to power, the manipulation of international affairs, the flowering of industry and even the much-criticized but nonetheless frequently brilliant conduct of the War to realize that the accepted categories of psychiatry do not apply here.

I have termed this book a work of propaganda and that word has highly egregious connotations, especially when used in connection with the National Socialists. "The people were deceived," cry the apologists but it comes with grace only from a real virgin. Joseph Goebbels, master propagandist, shows in his Foreword that he is well aware that his activity is often spurned as "dishonorable or inferior." Of course he calls this a case of mistaken identity. According to him, propaganda is, in fact, marked by truth and sincerity. At this juncture in history there is no need to verify that Nazi propaganda was mendacious, meretricious, manipulative and deceptive. A number of defendants at Nuremberg so testified. The operative question now is: It worked. Why did it work?

X A clever swayer of the masses realizes that he cannot *create* consumer demand. He must touch sentiment already existing. To some extent, he must tell the audience what it wants to hear. Goebbels said, "Propaganda simplifies and dramatizes truth so that it is intelligible and recognizable to the broad masses . . ." Take, for example, the "stab in the back" conceit explaining the World War I defeat, Hitler's main stock-in-trade at the outset of his public career—a simple, dramatic untruth but manifestly recognizable to the numerous ones who could not otherwise account for the downfall of the invincible Imperial Fatherland. Take the fact that Hitler fulminated against the "niggerization" of Germany and the people responded. He ended an interview with a reporter from a liberal newspaper with, "Now go back to Berlin and dance with your niggers." In 1928, there were 117 Negroes in all of Germany.

Most reliable of all targets was the anti-Semitic spook. It seems that when Jews could spare time from their primary occupation of ravishing flaxen-haired maidens, they managed to create Communism, "Kandinsky art," capitalism, corrupt German and pornography. Anti-Semitism has been known to have settled in mental grease traps before and after the Dictator.

As in all the essays, the Foreword proceeds from general observations to a description of Hitler's genius; in this case, his propaganda genius. "It is not well-known that in the early days of the Party for a long time (Hitler) occupied no other office than its Director of Propaganda and in his ingenious mastery and administration of this office of the Party he imprinted its real mental and organizational stamp on it." There are numerous puffed-up assertions in this book; this is not one of them. Proof lies in such propaganda triumphs as the wild enthusiasm at Party rallies and the number of opponents who were converted to sincere followers, convincing English authorities and newspapers that they were dealing with a man of peace. Germany's tone-setter never relinquished personal supervision of this activity, as Goebbels, of all people, was very well aware. Even at the Russian Front in critical times, he reviewed newspapers before status reports. He held image more important than substance and was ultimately hoisted on the petard of his true genius for propaganda.

Whence came this talent? Goebbels proposes an explanation: ". . . By his own nature and character he understood how to speak to the people, whose child he always was and always will be . . . This is a refrain throughout. A man of the masses, he could empathize with the masses and reach them.

We all know that Adolf Hitler came from humble beginnings. His extended family—grandparents, uncles, aunts, cousins—would have to be accounted severely disadvantaged. His father had succeeded in ascending the social ladder to the rank of an Austrian customs official, the highest civil service position available to a man of his education. His estate even provided a modest stipend to Adolf for about six years. Having dropped out of high school at Steyr, near his hometown Linz, at sixteen, the lad gravitated to Vienna when he was nineteen. There he struggled in the lower depths, never admitted to the professional schools of his choice, sleeping in flophouses for four years and never holding a steady job—it was against his principles. This misery was a function of his personality rather than of social station. His father was willing and able to support him at school and so was his widowed mother, for whom it was much more difficult. Whatever the reasons for the struggle of his early years, it was manifestly correct that he was born among the common people and had tasted bitter poverty in his life.

Thus far we have the story of young Abraham Lincoln. A Horatio Alger hero is always politically appealing. But if the Chief had risen from the masses, does it follow that he empathized and sympathized with them as claimed over and over by his associates here? Yes and no. From a propaganda standpoint, yes. With regard to truly benefiting the worker, a thousand times, no!

In the article by Joseph Goebbels on "The Führer as Orator," actually an extension of his initial remarks on propaganda, he expresses pride that the Leader and his Party reached people better than the Marxists (Social Democrats and Communists) who themselves, he says, proved capable of influencing public opinion during the "stab in the back"; and better than the center and right-wing groups whom he considered just plain dumb. Having read the formal orations in the Proceedings of the Reichstag under the Weimar Republic, I agree with Goebbels' estimate. They are far removed from ordinary concerns. A socialist commonwealth and even increased unemployment insurance is pie in the sky, for instance, to the man who has not had a job in four years. In contrast, the addresses of the national spokesman until 1942 were masterpieces of rapport with an audience. He was able to commune with them because he was one of them.

He did feel the fallen heart of the unemployed. There are so many tales of Hitler giving his coat to a jobless man even in this little volume, one is tempted to believe he was in the coat business. I guess he really did it more than once, not only as a neat public relations gesture, but out of fellow-feeling. More important, upon becoming Chancellor in 1933, he launched a massive public program designed to absorb all the jobless. The products of the program were far more socially useful than those of our W.P.A. for reasons which would be interesting to consider on another occasion), but any such approach hazards runaway inflation and excessive taxation. The War solved the problem for both Hitler and President Roosevelt but until it generated full employment, each man was willing to run the economic risks of federally financed work opportunities; each grasped the personal desolation and national peril of unemployment.

At that point, A.H. and F.D.R. parted company. The former had no concern to render secure the rights of the worker to pay and benefits; the latter did.

The American political system and its exigencies led to some support of unionism to fortify job rights of employees. The Nazis smashed the unions and dissolved them into an amalgam of management and labor, The German Work Front, described here by Labor Minister Robert Ley as, "an organization which includes all creative Germans, from the general manager to the apprentice."

That the Man from Austria, for all his rise from a log cabin to the White House, was not a friend of the common man is well limned by Prof. Arthur Schweitzer of Indiana University. "The Party and the State engaged in a deliberate institutional realignment of the prevailing labor markets . . . (by) fixing wage rates, prohibiting strikes and collective bargaining, imposing entry stipulations . . . emasculating unemployment insurance, regulating labor courts and imposing work books on laborers . . ." (BIG BUSINESS IN THE THIRD REICH, Indiana, 1965)

When we read Robert Ley in this book, the one-time chemist and heavyweight champion drinker illuminates how this was accomplished. It was through the establishment of a corporate state which encouraged loyalty at the expense of sub-group interests. This was, ironically, first propounded by the radical French Syndicalists and then by Italian fascism. It is to be expected that the Germans were most efficient of all about it. The afore-quoted Professor Schweitzer insists that sacrifices were all by labor; big business only profited. I believe he is generally right but underestimates some of the limitations on profit in the national interest.

It *is* worth noting that in this presentation, intended for popular consumption, managerial and machine employees were asked to submerge class concerns but not owners. Furthermore, Otto Dietrich does not mention the contributions of businessmen and industrialists though by birth and disposition he became one of the main pipelines to that community for the Nazis and arranged numerous parlor fund-raising gatherings of capitalists. National Socialist Hitler frequently assured listeners that he was out to preserve the economic system though this was mainly at private or even secret meetings and not published at the time.

Quoting the myth that "for many years the Führer himself was a manual laborer and experienced in his own body the pains and sufferings involved in working from morning to night in rain, wind and frost," Ley cites some of the benefits which only a person of that background could have conveyed to workers. Places of work were cleaned up; the "Beauty of Work" was one of their ubiquitous slogans. True. Another slogan, "Strength through Joy," represented a host of vacation tours and entertainments available at cheap rates to the working man and his family. Also true. (Incidentally, the slogans were posted in the concentration camps.) However, the bread and circuses could at any time be withdrawn by the emperor; they were privileges, not rights.

The link between the Leader and the common people is to be sought not in true benefits for workers or anything meriting the name National *Socialist* but in a mutual passion described by Friedrich Nietzsche as "Resentment." It was later elaborated, particularly in French sociology. Nietzsche claimed that this sentiment motivated Judaism and Christianity, religions of resentful slaves, to impose a slave mentality of morality on the open, free and noble Germanic mentality. The sociologists discerned Nietzsche's "Resentment" (they interpreted it in the theory of "Ressentiment") as a basic attitude of the dispossessed. This book lays hammer blows on "the rich who could not read our pain" or "the depraved advocates of glass-enclosed skyscrapers" or "Marxist despoilers of the nation's sense of honor." When Hitler spoke like this, as he did, he touched a sensitive spot and could say "we" as no aristocrat could.

Everyone was subordinate to the State. The State was an impersonal entity. It was personalized in Adolf Hitler. He was idolized as the apogee of all virtue and talent. That was the meaning and purpose of this book when it was originally distributed in Germany in 1936.

In connection with this overriding purpose, the two-paragraph contribution of Hermann Göring hits the center mark. It is an excerpt from an introduction of the Führer to a session of the Reichstag convened at Nuremberg rather than in the regular Berlin chamber on September 15, 1935. Its tone is no less than religious as befits a god. "All our thanks to you, our love for you and our glowing trust in you, my Führer, shines forth today from hundreds of thousands of eyes . . . in you there has arisen for this people not only a Führer but also a Savior."

It is strange, in a way, that Göring delivered this highflown liturgy. In conversation he was blunt, direct, the very opposite of "churchy." Nor would he have heard much of this style of talk in his adult life, having a real aversion for services. The answer is obvious. This speech, as all his speeches, was ghostwritten. The only extant statements of Hermann Göring which actually came from him are his dirty jokes at Cabinet meetings transcribed by a conscientious stenographer. Even the dialogue that was attributed to him at the time in newspapers was edited. He was a man of tremendous accomplishments but not of words.

However, the Air Force Marshal was too shrewd to have submitted anything in his name without reading it. He and the entire elite understood the necessity of making Hitler a semi-divine focus for the nation with superhuman powers of direction and the authority to resolve internal differences.

For the volume in hand, the participation of Göring, even in a most minimal way, was an *imprimatur*. He was number-two man in the country in fact by 1935 and this was formalized several years later. He had supervised actions of huge consequence in internal affairs, rearmament and foreign relations. Hitler, himself high-strung and requiring an enormous effort of will to make decisions, left no doubt about his admiration for his portly associate and the reason. (Read this carefully. It will tell you something significant about both men.) "The Reich's Marshal is brutal and ice-cold in crises. I've always noticed that when it's a question of facing up to a decision he is ruthless and hard as iron. You'll get nobody better than him, you couldn't find anybody better. He's gone through all the crises with me, the toughest crises, and was ice-cold. Whenever the going was really hard, he turned ice-cold. . ." (Joachim C. Fest, HITLER, New York, 1973)

Göring said his *te laudamus*; did he really mean it? Probably not. In the two well-disciplined published repentances of Albert Speer, we derive a picture of the World War I air hero calculatingly joining the tiny National Socialist Party in 1921, not out of specific conviction, but because it offered the most promising vehicle, precisely because so raw, for ultimately attaining power and glory. Göring did not surmount his pragmatic motivation throughout his long, distinguished service to the Party and State and was fully aware of Hitler's shortcomings as a god, having dragged him by the forelock into crucial decisions.

"Play all the sad songs you want for the bridegroom; he has his own happy thoughts in mind." The contributors to this volume are most happy with the miracle of their rise to power. It was the world and all for them, especially those who had come from nowhere. As one new officeholder told Hermann Rauschning, "I don't want to fall back down. Maybe you can bide your time. You're not sitting in any fire. But I've been unemployed, do you hear! Before I go through that again I'll turn criminal. I'm staying on top, no matter what. We won't climb up twice." (GESPRÄCHE MIT HITLER, Zurich, 1940) The legions of Roehm had been subdued by bloodletting and they were the types most candidly elated at the victory. As one of them who walked into the office of his new boss, Kurt W. Luedecke, happily exclaimed, "Hi there, Luedecke! Terrific! I'm a big shot!" (I KNEW HITLER, New York, 1937) But even in 1936 and even for the less primitive, it was an ecstatic recollection.

In his third article, "The Führer as Statesman," Joseph Goebbels declares, "[The resurrection of Germany] is the result of a statesmanly evolution from the seven-man party in Munich to the Great Power status of the German Reich. There are a number of decisions included in this evolution. Altogether they produce a picture of a fabulous and fantastic rise which will be exalted by later historians unquestionably as the greatest political miracle of the 20th century."

This essay actually gives a picture of the tactical adroitness which produced the Party's triumph rather than what is usually termed statesmanship. Yet, the prestigious title, "The Führer and the National Socialist Movement," so prominent in the minds and hearts of Party people, was assigned to the relatively less known Philipp Bouhler. Bouhler was by no means insignificant. Like every one of the contributors except Fritz Todt, he was a veteran of the earliest crusade. To be an "Old Battler" in itself gave entrée to the Chief and that was an enormous source of influence. Bouhler also rose to prominence in the paramilitary governmental structure and, by 1939, occupied a position equivalent to lieutenant-general. He was placed in charge of the controversial euthanasia program in that year, along with the chiropractor who tended Hitler medically. He was no Goebbels nor is his article anywhere near as effective as that of the Propaganda Minister. Goebbels is vivid, forceful and free about mentioning matters which Bouhler would have considered embarrassing. Goebbels tells of the determination, when the National Socialists moved onto the national stage, to destroy the bourgeois political parties. He does not tell, though everyone knew, that Hitler was at the same time assuring those parties that he wanted them to survive and become his partners. Bouhler sounds like a city hospital superintendent imploring the commissioner for more toothpaste. He is very guarded.

We have no way of knowing why these particular contributors were chosen and who designated their topics. In some cases the reason is obvious. If it was decided to feature the Autobahn, who else but Todt should write (an excellent article)? Or maybe the choice of man preceded the decision on topic. In the case in point about the rise of the Party, the reason is not obvious. I speculate that Bouhler, as an old and trusted friend, was chosen by his mentor for some obscure goal in Party chess and because Hitler wished to be certain that he personally would set the tone. The writing bears traces of his incredibly convoluted style and we have already remarked on his obsession with public relations. I suspect, too, that he had much input from general conception to, in his manner, the color of the cover. However, I have no solid evidence for these guesses.

One is tempted to speculate on dignitaries who did not write articles, such as Hess. Goebbels and Göring, too, always had reservations about him, considering him rather odd. They turned out to be wrong. Hess is very odd. Again, lacking knowledge of the circumstances, such detection is idle. Maybe the man was out of town at the time.

There is one omission which does bear scrutiny. There is little in this book about Jews. Anti-Semitism was the keystone of Hitler's whole world outlook and every one of his associates, including Mary Poppins Speer, came to him already equipped with this hatred, so how could they write a book bearing his name as a title and be almost silent on the subject?

The policy had to be deliberate. Having foresworn guesswork on why certain dignitaries did not write for the book, I shall now guess why Julius Streicher is not represented. After all, as a former schoolteacher, he was one of the more educated ones. I believe the reason is that he was so corroded with anti-Semitism that he could not have restrained himself and rather than having an awkward dispute over his essay, none was requested.

William Shirer explains why, in 1936, there might have been such an anomaly. "The Olympic games held in Berlin in August 1936 afforded the Nazis a golden opportunity to impress the world with the achievements of the Third Reich and they made the most of it. The signs *Juden unerwünscht* (Jews Not Welcome) were quietly hauled down from the shops, hotels, beer gardens and places of public entertainment, the persecution of the Jews and of the two Christian churches temporarily halted, and the country put on its best behavior." (William Shirer, THE RISE AND FALL OF THE THIRD REICH, New York, 1960) A footnote adds, "The author was violently attacked in the German press and on the radio, and threatened with expulsion, for having written a dispatch saying that some of these anti-Semitic signs were being removed for the duration of the Olympic games." (ibid.)

Toward the end of his career, Hitler became so obsessed with killing Jews that he sacrificed part of the War effort to murdering my brothers and sisters. But in 1936 he was still capable of concealing his enmity, if necessary.

The original of this volume was published in the northern city of Altona, near Hamburg, in 1936, judging by internal evidence. Its pages are larger than in most books, about like *Time* magazine, but spacing and type-size reduces the number of words. It is neat but inexpensive. Its printing is clean and correct; its thin, hard covers cased onto the body and finished with frugal duckcloth (brown, of course); its illustrations in the form of clear, excellently produced photographs attached apart from the printing process. The publisher is "Cigarette Photo Service." That, and the matter of the separately attached photographs, has led to speculation on its origin. Cigarette manufacturers or more often their trade association, mostly located in North Germany, used to distribute pictures of soccer players as a premium with their products, like American baseball cards with bubble gum. When the entire series had been collected, consumers were entitled to a printed book appearing much like ADOLF HITLER with spaces for the cards. Perhaps, then, someone had the bright idea of applying the same technique to politics and this is another instance of the cooperation between businessmen and Nazis. The first run of the soccer book was 250,000 and they were always reprinted.

Anyone who has read popular German writing on Hitler in all the media at that time will have been struck by their essential sameness. It is as if they were all operating from the same press release and who knows? Here we are reading a classic specimen of such propaganda. It is a particular which illuminates the general.

Those responsible for this republication will be gratified if it proves of value to scholars. Its aim, though, is to the average person. Here is information on how the Nazis sought to influence the Germans. Similar methods are being employed today in South Africa, Uganda, Brazil and at least nine other countries. Can it happen here? That is the question—can it happen here?

You are about to read material shedding fresh light on a bloody event in history. The book ADOLF HITLER surely does not tell the truth. It ought to be read in order to search out the whole truth.

In 1933 the critic Ernst Bertram wrote a "Fire Song," music to burn books by, sending a copy to his "dear friend," the self-exiled Thomas Mann so that the latter "might better understand." It concluded, "Because I love the Fatherland/I outlaw all that seduces her/Into the flames with what threatens her!" Thomas Mann did not answer personally, but also wrote a poem. It concluded, "Because I love the Fatherland/I cannot see her burn the search for truth/Along with it, her soul perishes in the flames."

RABBI JULIUS ROSENTHAL

My Führer, we are not able to express our thanks in words. Nor can we document in words our loyalty and admiration for you. All our thanks to you, our love for you and our glowing trust in you, my Führer, shines forth today from hundreds of thousands of eyes.

Today, a whole people, a whole nation feels strong and happy because in you there has arisen for this people not only a Führer but also a Savior.

HERMANN GÖRING
President of the Reichstag
Given before the German Reichstag at Nuremberg.
September 15, 1935

Foreword

Throughout the world today and even in Germany there is a great deal of misunderstanding about the notion of Propaganda. Since these misunderstandings are very deep-rooted and mostly based on prejudices, they are very difficult to correct. Yet since the end of the War, the German people have had in this regard the benefit of an instructive lesson that could not be any better or more impressive. Historically speaking, in a very short time, Propaganda has proved to be a powerful instrument of the first order in Germany. Today no further proof is required than the fact that Imperial Germany met its downfall under the assault of Marxist Propaganda, and the Marxist-Democratic regime was also removed, since it was opposed not only by the Nationalist Socialist idea, but also by National Socialist Propaganda with a new order and a talent that were superior.

Also Propaganda must be understood. It is of no avail at all merely to commandeer a few clever heads as occasion demands. Like every great art, Propaganda has its people who are especially capable in the field; they found a particular school of thought and training schools follow. We must also dismiss the widespread error that maintains that there is something dishonorable or inferior about it. It happens that Propaganda is situated in life and deals practically with the world of appearances. But it has nothing to do with advertising. It allows the best things and persons to speak for themselves, and it takes great care that if something worthwhile is found, its full worth is also described and illustrated.

In this case good things and great men do their own work. People then have to bring themselves without narrow-mindedness to allow words to come naturally. Therefore, the most important characteristic of especially successful Propaganda is that it leave out nothing, but also add nothing which does not pertain to the essence of the subject in question. The characteristic traits of conditions or personalities must be clearly, penetratingly and very simply and artlessly drawn out of the entangled nonessentials, so that it is intelligible and recognizable to the broad masses who must be recruited and whose enthusiasm must be aroused.

For this art National Socialism and its chief deputies have brought not only a natural talent, but in their persistent work and indefatigable and close contact with the people they have learned and made use of the most progressive and highest refinement. The Führer himself was its great teacher. It is not well known that in the early days of the Party for a long time he occupied no other office than its leader of Propaganda, and in his ingenious mastery and administration of this office of the Party he imprinted its real mental and organizational stamp on it. Since by his own nature and character he understood how to speak to the people, whose child he always was and always will be, and to perform his tasks from the heart, the whole love and the colossal support of the trust of his disciples and later of the German people became concentrated on his person. The masses then saw him from the distance at first only as a politician and statesman. His purely human aspect frequently remained in the background.

Today he is known by the whole world as the creator of National Socialist teaching and the builder of the National Socialist State, as the pioneer of a new European Order and the Guide to peace and well-being for the peoples. But behind this knowledge, untold millions of men throughout the world have a possibly still unclear presentiment of the persuasiveness and fascination of the man Adolf Hitler. The great simplicity and simple greatness that his person radiates impress not only every German but also every instinctively thinking foreigner, penetrating and convincing them. Today he can be for the whole world the man to be appealed to, the one who is rooted in the deepest and clearest way in the feelings and thoughts of modern times, and therefore the one who like no one else has within himself the capacity to grant to this time of ours a new shape and form.

In order fully to understand him in this dimension, one must know him not only as a politician and statesman but as a man. This then is the purpose of this book. It is evidence of his very personality that is brought forward with love and honor by his closest collaborators and oldest battle companions. Here they use their words to publicize a picture of this great man, a picture which heretofore has not existed in this form. They have all known the Führer for many years and they have learned every day to admire him more and more. This is the real value of this book.

The Führer appears here as a person in direct relation to all the questions that are of interest to our time. Happily the German people will grab at this opportunity to see the Führer at close hand and therefore also come closer to him personally.

It is especially fortunate that an opportunity is offered to acquire this book in an easy and inexpensive way, which in turn will give broad access to the masses of German readers. May this be the beginning of a happy and successful venture for the German people.

DR. JOSEPH GOEBBELS

Through his example, the Führer promotes air travel.

The Führer Traveling

By the late SS Brigade Leader Julius Schreck

Never has there been a traveling statesman who so thoroughly got to know his country and his people as Adolf Hitler. Whether in automobiles, planes or trains, his trips always helped him become thoroughly acquainted with his people.

Even at the beginning of his movement he had the foresight to recognize the importance of the medium of rapid transportation, especially the car, which he used despite the fact that it was not customary at the time. Even today, the Führer still prefers the car, since he feels it important to keep in constant contact with his fellow countrymen and the veteran members of the Party.

As the great political power struggles had shown, through motorization the Führer was far ahead of all his opponents. At that time the Führer was never jostled and crowded by enthusiasts. During these years of struggle, we made very many trips and the going was very difficult. It was only through the presence of mind of authority that we were able to win out in the fighting. But the Führer could not be restrained by any alarming news whatsoever from travelling to the strongholds of his Red and Black opponents, often right into the midst of the remote centers of the Bolshevik organizations and even to the very demonstrations of the Blacks themselves. Many times our car

At the Monument to the Fallen in Hiltpoltstein (Fränkische Schweiz).

was completely surrounded by thousands of agitated fellow countrymen. But it always happened that at the Führer's gaze the raised fists suddenly relaxed as the people looked up and realized that this Hitler was quite different from the one that had always been described to them. How many bewildered German workers for the first time looked into the eyes of the man who ought to have been their opponent, and at once became fanatical followers of his Movement. Neither newspaper propaganda nor books achieved this miracle alone. Thus three years after he took power, he could say: "Where is there a statesman like me in the world who after only three years of rule has nothing to fear when he goes out among his people?"

Today, when his work and his government duties allow, the Führer does not sit behind in his office, but goes out into the country to meet the people. He sits in his Mercedes and suddenly turns up in this place or that: one day in the Ruhr district, another in Baden, Württemberg, Saxony, East Prussia, on the Seaboard . . . in fact there is no district he has not visited at least once. At the steering wheel, behind the windshield I suddenly hear astonished and enthusiastic cries: "It's Hitler!" or "The Führer is here!" Often people do not notice at all who is motoring through the town. When the motorcade had passed through, the three black cars attracted people's attention and then it became clear to them who it was who had motored by. Later, in similar circumstances, people began to race along with the car, the passage through the street became narrowed by the crowd to an almost alarming extent, and finally we had to stop very frequently so the Führer could give his hand to the excited people and receive flowers, or also, as in one instance, sign a few postcards.

Who is there like me who has had ten years of good fortune to be constantly so close to the Führer, and to live with him on his many journeys? Thousands of unforgettable pictures remain with me from over the years. Out of these trips we get an unshakeable belief in the German people and it is so very heartwarming when you are lucky enough to have the experience of these many days.

The Führer takes long trips only in an open car, and even when it rains he leaves the top down if the trip is an official one. To the advice of his

On his trip through Germany the Führer uses an open car.

Julius Schreck—May 16, 1936.

The Party's Farewell To Julius Schreck

Today, the National Socialist Movement takes leave of Julius Schreck. It takes leave of one of its oldest and truest. It takes leave of one of its best and most irreplaceable. It takes leave of one of its most unassuming, a man who wanted nothing for himself, and who gave everything for Germany and the Führer.

Wherever fighting for Germany mattered, he was there at the front, both abroad in the World War and at home.

Boundless was his respect and his love for the Führer; tireless his concern for the Führer; circumspect was his thoughtfulness for the Führer's personal safety.

To the last his nature radiated trustworthiness. In the hard times of battle his presence instilled a feeling of security in his Party comrades.

Unflinching was his judgment of men; his affection was as unconcealed as his aversion. A rough broadsword with a warm heart. Feared by opponents, loved by all who counted him as one of them, honored as a fatherly friend by his subordinates.

He had the good fortune to enjoy his Führer's confidence. The Movement lowers its banners at the last salute to Julius Schreck. In doing so, it swears that his breed and his spirit will be an example to the young men on the way up, and that in this way he will still serve the Movement far into the future, for the prosperity of our great National Socialist Germany.

RUDOLF HESS

A trip through the Harz Mountains: the Führer too can be gay.

Rest in the woods.

On the train.

In a German landscape. Hiltpoltstein.

The Führer reads the itinerary thoroughly.

The Führer in Franconia.

escorts he always had the same answer: "As long as the Storm Troopers and the other service people have to stand in the rain, we too can get wet." Thousands witnessed how he, bareheaded and clad in his brown shirt, led the march of the Storm Troopers on the occasion of the return of the Saar, how at the Stralsund election campaign, after a 3 a.m. flight, he spoke to the waiting crowds in the pouring rain, or how he journeyed in the rain through Holstein to the Adolf Hitler polder and, soaking wet, without a thought for himself, spoke to the Storm Troopers as they too stood in the rain.

Even in his very first car he always sat next to the driver. Today, after fifteen years of chauffeuring him, he, though Reich's Chancellor still takes the same seat. The Führer decides on the travel route himself and loves to use side roads and experience the German landscape off the beaten track.

Earlier, it was even simpler, since the Führer was not as well known as he is today. At that time we were often able to spend the night or take a meal in an inn without being recognized. Today things are different. The news of the Führer's coming spreads like wildfire throughout the towns and villages where our path will lead. In their joy, many use the radio to inform the next village, and then the inhabitants who have never seen the Führer are there to greet Hitler, waiting for the car to arrive. These were such uplifting experiences and I often wished I were a poet so I could find the words to describe skilfully the thousands of little incidents as we experienced them.

Once we drove through a place and everybody was out, old and young, the clubs and the schools,

mothers with children in their arms. The main street was quickly transformed into a sea of banners. Girls from the *Bund deutscher Mädchen* tried to bring the car to a stop, but time was pressing. The Führer had to be at another destination at a given time, where hundreds of thousands were waiting for him at a mass meeting. All of a sudden a big, muscular man jumped out of the crowd and onto the radiator of the car. At this point the Führer had to slow down, since the car was already surrounded by all the inhabitants of the place. Each one wanted to shake the Führer's hand. Women with babes in arms could not reach him. They held up their little ones, Germany's future, over the heads of the enthusiastic crowd, as if they wanted to say: You belong to him!

In describing great men, we also must see the small touches of concern in their lives. Here is one among hundreds of episodes. It is near 10 p.m. as the Führer's car was going in the direction of Würzburg to a special march-in-review in Meiningen. There in the light of the headlights were two Storm Troopers. The Führer had the car stop. They were asked where they were going. "To the next railway station. My comrade can't walk any more and we still have three hours to go." "Get in!" They did not have the slightest idea whose guests they were. We talked generalities and asked whether they had ever seen the Führer. "Yes, today at the march." The car stopped. We had reached our destination. The Führer, who was sitting in front, called to them and pushed some money into each man's hand. There in the dark of night, a small light was shining on the Führer's face. Both Storm Troopers were struck dumb.

On a ride through Germany.

At the Wartburg.

Pleasure trip through Germany.

With the D-2600 over Nuremberg. Arrival at the
Reich's Party Day, 1934.

Wasn't it the Führer who was speaking with them? Yes, it was he! No word passed their lips because of their great joy and awe. I stepped on the gas and the Mercedes moved on in the dark night. When we reached a turn in the road, we saw the two men still standing where we had left them on the highway, still not recovered from their experience.

The great and difficult election campaign of that time claimed a great deal of the Führer's time and so he made use of airplanes to get about, and this at a time when people did not have much confidence in the air service. Weeks on end the plane flew him from town to town, without concern for wind or weather.

When I look back on this period I feel goose bumps, remembering the many flights at night in squalls and clouds. One instance speaks for itself. During the time of the election campaign, the terminus of the flight departure was changed. Yet

The Führer in an airplane.

At Bückeberg for the Harvest Festival in 1934.

*Women from Bückeberg in their holiday dress
at the Harvest Festival, 1934.*

each of the special mass meetings—and there were many in various cities of Germany in one day—were all on time.

Often people would urge the Führer not to take a particular flight. This, however, was always his answer: "When need be, then I too shall fly in a storm." How the opposition papers would have capitalized on it if the set flight plan had not been followed or if a scheduled meeting had not been held.

I remember especially one particular flight from Fürth to Frankfurt. The old Rohrbach, the first plane ever used by the Führer, was moored with fuel tanks. A storm was raging all over Germany with an intensity that had seldom been seen. All planes were grounded. It was even difficult to stand up. Everyone shook his head when the Führer boarded the plane. After a few moments it struggled to get aloft. The plane flew off with great difficulty through thunder and rainbows, storms and snows. The plane often tipped from side to side and many a flying companion of the Führer's struck his head on the cabin roof, but there were no major mishaps. One time the plane had to make an unscheduled emergency landing far from its destination. The meeting in Kiel was to have begun at 8 o'clock. About 5 o'clock I received the news that the Führer had had to land in Travemünde, where there was a low ceiling, along with clouds and a raging storm. Immediately the motorcade rushed off in the direction of Lübeck, and at Eutin, we met the Führer, who had come there himself in a rented car, and brought him straight to Kiel. Although for reasons of time the Führer today sometimes uses the railways for night trips, he still stresses his great love for the automobile, about which he himself once said that it opened up Germany for him. He was also very fond of his Ju 52, which was under the command of Flight-Captain SS Oberführer Baur, one of the first real artists among the flight captains. The greatest thing for the Führer is when, after the strain of weeks of work, he can take to his car again and motor through the German countryside. The finest days for me are when I am sitting behind the wheel and driving the Führer through the happy and peaceful country, just as I once did years ago in times of struggle and want.

On a trip through East Prussia, the Führer visits a farming family.

The Führer and the German People

By Dr. Otto Dietrich

The relationship of the German people with the Führer is always a continued source of joyful pride for Germans, and for foreigners a cause for amazement and surprise. Nowhere in the world is there such a fanatical love on the part of millions of men for one man, yet this love is not exaggerated or delirious. It is the consequence of a deep and great faith, an unlimited trust, as children often have for a good and kind father.

Enthusiasm wanes after a few years. This love, however, comes from deep inside one's innermost being. Once it rises, it is imperishable and lasts for centuries. It is like a large, powerful lamp that never loses its intensity. This love does not suddenly burst into flame, and is not enkindled by startling and inspiring incidents. Rather it grows slowly and impressively. It does not appear with some furious impetuosity on one single occasion. It is always there, at every moment and with every

German. For special reasons it fills his heart with pride. It may be present in a crowd with hundreds of thousands of fellow countrymen when the Führer appears before them. But it needs no external motive to be present, and it is there even when one is alone at his place of work. When anyone ever thinks of the Führer, there always rises up within him this deep love and it alone is justification for the phrase: "Hitler is Germany—Germany is Hitler." Never has there been a man who was closer to the heart of the people than this man, who himself rose out of that very people. He did not come from the outside. He was born in the people, saw their needs and lived their life. And if anyone today should ask about the name of the German "Unknown Soldier," the whole German people would answer: Adolf Hitler!

He is the conscience of the nation; from him the pain and also the defiance of an enslaved people

17

On the day of the return of the Saar.

Enthusiasm over the Führer's presence in Hamburg harbor.

A delegation from the Saar in front of the Reich's Chancery.

Even the farmer believes in the Führer.

Everybody wants to shake the Führer's hand at least once.

She wants the Führer's hand.

Age trusts the Führer.

cried out. In him would be the Life's Will of all Germany, in the hour of her deepest humiliation in word and deed. [Adolf Hitler never uttered anything other than what the people thought in their deepest soul; he never did anything other than what the whole people wanted to do. He never was, is not, and never will be a Dictator who forces his personal opinions or his longing for domination on the people. Truly, he is only the Führer, and that is the highest thing that can ever be said of a person. This is why the people love him so, why they have confidence in him, why they are so unspeakably happy with this

man, because, for the first time in their history, they can all become truly themselves.]

Here lies the secret of the imperishability of Adolf Hitler and his work, the guarantee of the immutability of the direction that he has taken; then it is no longer the man Adolf Hitler, no longer his work, no longer his direction, but the German people themselves who are expressing themselves in him. In him they love themselves; in him they follow their secret wishes; in him they bring their bravest thoughts to reality. Each individual knows this and therefore Adolf Hitler is a stranger to no one, nor is anyone a stranger to the

A picture from the 1932 election campaign in Hesse.

Führer. He speaks with workers and farmers, Nobel Prize winners and artists, champions and dreamers, the lucky and the despairing, and each one hears his own speech, understands and is understood. Everything is spontaneous and manifest and no one is shy before the great man. No one is commandeered, no one is coaxed, but each is called, just as he was called, by his own conscience, and this is nothing left for him to do but to follow so that he will not feel guilty and unhappy in his own heart. He freely does what must be done, and there is no people on earth freer than the German people.

Therefore the people never tire of listening to the Führer's words and if the Reich's Party Day in Nuremberg had lasted twice as long, the people would still be listening as attentively to his last words as they did to his first. He could go on and on traveling without stopping throughout Germany, and the people would look forward every day to seeing him, and rejoice on the last day as they did on the first, bringing him their children to show him the future of Germany. When necessary, they also give him their lives, as hundreds of his Party comrades did in the years of the struggle.

There were emperors and kings, monarchs and

folk heroes, usurpers and tyrants, clever and great rulers over the people, but never before was there such a person as the Führer. This happens only once in the world, and this is the good fortune that has fallen to the German people. As long as this is not understood, people can understand nothing about the German people. No one can comprehend why eyes light up, voices shout with joy, arms fly up, hearts beat swiftly, when Adolf Hitler walks before the German people. And these external signs are only the visible expression of the permanent and mysterious relationship that exists between people and Führer; Hitler again creates the force for a new task, just as the people derive strength and create it from his appearance.

This is very specially evident when the German Youth and the Führer stand together. And the longer a person has been near the Führer, accompanying him over days, weeks and months, the more unforgettable are the images that rise to the surface.

Once, midway on the main road between Stettin and Pasewalk, a good 10 kilometers from a village, the Führer met some German Youth during a rainstorm. Somehow they had got wind that on that day the Führer would be passing along at this point. It was evening, and as the Führer's car with both escort cars finally sped along the highway, far in the distance, in the trees alongside the road, a crowd could already be seen, and then as the cars came closer there were multitudes of banner-waving children. They were setting off colored fireworks, red, blue and green; sentinels were posted before the head troop so that with hand movements the motorcade would be brought to a halt. Although time was exceedingly tight, the Führer gave the command to stop, and in a moment the cars were surrounded by a hundred children who not only sprang onto the running boards but even piled onto the radiator and the hood, so as to see through the windshield where the Führer was inside the car. After the three cars of the motorcade had been examined in turn, an especially resourceful boy discovered the Führer. He shouted out: "Here he is! Everybody come here!" And now pandemonium . . . The escort command had to intervene, because a few of the boys were trying to hang on to the swaying canvas cover. The leader of the young troop, the same one who had discovered the Führer, asked to give a short speech, young, fresh and unperturbed, and then made room for a white-clad girl. She curtsied low and spoke in her own verses of the young people's joy in seeing the Führer. At the end, the child presented Adolf Hitler with a small basket of splendid rosy-cheeked apples. Deeply touched, the Führer stroked the blond hair, whereupon the child, out of her extreme good fortune and great joy, began to weep. Then the motorcade slowly detached itself from the swarm of children and drove away, seeing through the rear window the flag-waving little figures making their farewells.

At all times and in every demonstration it is the youth that is in the forefront. They are well-behaved and modest, just as their teacher or Wolf Cub leader had taught them to be, standing in a straight row and not in some haphazard formation. But there are others, the daring, who hang from the branches of trees, sit on the monuments and building façades or stand like an avenue of living statues on high factory walls, and climb flagpoles and lampposts. When the Führer finally comes along, the air is filled with unending shouts of joy. The favorite places for the young people to wait for the Führer are always sharp curves, which become sharper still when they line up at them to make the cars move as slowly as possible. A still better place, certainly, is a building site on the highway where it is very sure that the Führer can only drive by at walking speed and people can then catch sight of him no matter what. This almost always causes some real difficulties for the cars to pass. The crowd itself forms a lane and then the children run from the end of the car to the front so as to block the path again with their renewed jubilation.

One evening in a city in southern Germany ten thousand Hitler Youth formed a lane in the street at a demonstration in honor of the Führer. Every time the cars got underway, the distance between the walls of people became narrower, so that ultimately only just enough room remained to let the car through. All of a sudden, however, there was a lot of rushing, crowding and pushing, although the boys carrying the torches standing in the front row tried to hold the crowd back. Instead, they were dragged along and began swinging the torches and shouting, shining them inside the cars, showing their enthusiasm for the Führer and his entourage, who received audible testimony of love and a hardy portion of smoke to swallow. It was fortunate that they did not set the cars on fire. After a quarter of an hour, the Führer succeeded in freeing himself from this enthusiastic group of young people.

It is amusing to see with what earnestness and eagerness the young people endeavor to photograph the Führer. They stand with their tiny cameras, their fingers on the shutter button, trembling with nervousness and excitement. These cameras must bring much happiness when they finally succeed in taking a picture. An astonishingly large number of good pictures come out of all this patience. And luck seems to be with the young people, while on the other hand amateur photographers often bemoan the fact that they are incapable of matching the collective enthusiasm and of seizing the most favorable opportunity.

In one place, in a trip through Upper Silesia, the Führer was greeted and a little girl had the honor of presenting him with a bouquet of flowers. With it a short poem was to be recited. She said the first line but then in the excitement lost her train of thought and after looking around more or less helplessly, she suddenly took the flowers, stretched herself up on tiptoes to the Führer, put the flowers in his hand and said: "Hitler, here you are . . . I forgot everything." At that she ran away.

A street is shut off. Men are standing pressed closely together. They are waiting, already waiting for many hours—they are waiting for the Führer. They want to see him. They all want to see him, men, women, boys and girls. "It's like a holiday today," says an old lady, and right she is when the Führer comes to this little town for the first time.

From roofs and gables flags were blowing, and over the streets garlands were strung. The whole town has put on its festive dress. And then the Führer comes . . . A whirlwind seems to be going through the crowds. Here and there a trafic director can be seen, but the pushing and shoving persisted. Arms were raised towards the Führer. People were laughing and crying, expressing their joy

and enthusiasm. Women raised their children in their arms over the crowd, extending their little arms, and with beaming eyes and smiling mouths they chimed in with the enthusiastic "Heil Hitler!" of the crowd. Filled with trust and faith, the women and mothers looked up at the Führer. They know that only he is to be thanked for the fact that their unemployed husbands have again found work. Work and therefore bread for the family. Life had meaning again, and they could look to the future without fear and anxiety.

Then there is a letter which a girl, serving her compulsory year on the land, wrote to her parents: "I just have to write to you . . . What I am now writing will please you, I know. Just think, dear parents, I have seen the Führer. Reflect on it, the Führer. . . ."

How much there is in these words: "Reflect on it, the Führer"! How brightly shines the pride of the experience. How great is the love of this child of the German people for her Führer! Here is the fulfillment of a wish, which will fortify this girl with great courage.

It is a real gift of fate to her during her year on the land—the most beautiful gift possible—a

A visit to a victim of the Reinsdorf catastrophe.

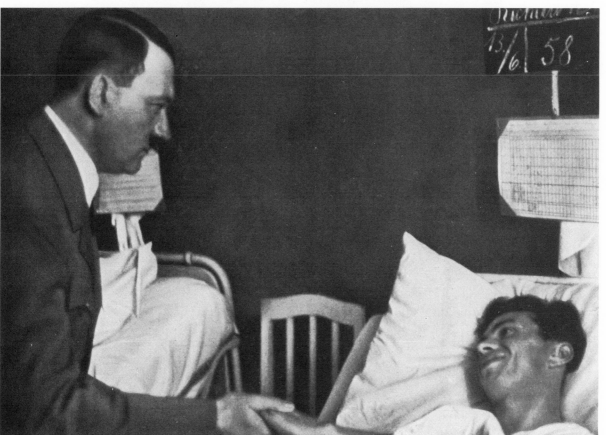

A Saar rally at Ehrenbreitstein in August, 1934.

meeting with the Führer. "Think what that means . . ."

And everywhere it is the same: in Bavaria and East Prussia, in Silesia and the Rhineland.

 On a highway in the Palatinate, two workers were walking to the next town. Their work camp was far in the country and the way to the railway station was a long one. But both men are happy with fortitude, and happy too that they were on their way to a vacation in their homes after months of healthy and strenuous work. They were singing together "In the homeland . . . in the homeland . . ." when a motorcade came up to them. "They have it fine," said one. "They are quicker than we," said the other. "They're beckoning to us," they both said in unison. And the motorcade stopped and waited until the two men it had put on the run could catch up with it. "Where are you coming from? Where are you going? Get in!" They were both wide-eyed with astonishment that someone would stop on the highway and offer men on work detail a ride. And that someone was the Führer. He let them tell him about themselves and describe their life, with de-

24

*Minister Darré greets the Führer on the occasion of
the Harvest Thanksgiving Festival.*

tails about their work service camp, which he was
anxious to know. Then they arrived in the little
town. The cars stopped. As a farewell the Führer
asked one of the two: "It is going to rain. Do you
have a coat with you?" "I have no civilian coat,
my Führer. I was too long without work." Then
the Führer took his own gray travel coat and hung
it around the shoulders of his fellow countryman.
And before he could utter a word of thanks, the
motorcade sped off.

Somewhere a band of young workers were fall-
ing in for roll call. The Führer passed them in review and looked at each one of the young men
straight in the eye. He turned to one of the young
workers: "Are you a Party member?" "No." "Are
you a Storm Trooper?" "No, I belong to the Work
Front." "Where were you then before that?" the
Führer asked after a pause. The blond young man
lowered his eyes, straightened up and said hesi-
tatingly: "I was a Young Communist, my Führer!"
The words were obviously difficult for him. All
eyes were upon him. A painful moment. Then the
Führer took the young man's hand, pressed it and
said laughingly: "But today you are all with me,

boys." And with a beet-red face the young worker answered: "By God, you can depend on that, my Führer!"

These scenes can be repeated over and over again, showing the relationship of the German people with Adolf Hitler.

In Hamburg, at a demonstration for the Führer on the evening before a crucial public meeting, a disabled soldier and his son broke through the cordon which barred entrance to the Führer's quarters: "I want to serenade the Führer." The SS men let the man through and he found himself on the street beneath the Führer's window. With trembling fingers he drew his instrument out of its grey case and played a song. The many thousands in the crowd listened quietly and attentively. The plaintive melodies of the street musician reached the Führer and he listened to the playing. He allowed the man to come up to him, spoke to him and heard the story of his life. "Four years I have been without work," said the disabled soldier. "Could you, my Führer, get me a job in your service?" The Führer motioned to one of his assistants. There were two quick telephone conversations, and then the Führer said: "Report tomorrow to such and such a place. You can begin work immediately." With lightning speed the news spread through the waiting crowd. Unwilling to stop the demonstration, the people continued their ovations in answer to the Führer.

Unforgettable, too, was the day when the Führer appeared at the burial of the victims of the terrible and catastrophic Reinsdorf explosion. The coffins of the fallen work heroes stood in long rows. Flags flew at half-mast, dark crepe was hung, and the funeral congregation stood by in silence. The nearest relatives of the deceased were gathered together in a special place. It was a picture of boundless sorrow, with weeping mothers, sisters, brothers and fathers. The Führer appeared and the service began. The grief of the relatives was heart rending. The orators and clergymen spoke, the song of the good comrade rang out and honor salvos rolled across the field. Then the Führer left his attendants and walked alone across the square to the relatives. Seeking consolation, a hundred arms stretched out to him and whoever was there had indelibly printed on his memory the grief-stricken face of the Führer as he now stood in the midst of the suffering mourners. Then he began to speak with the individual men and women or shook their hands silently. The circle around him became narrower and narrower. Tears ran dry, and men who had lost control regained their composure. Here the Führer took in his consoling hands the head of a disconsolate old woman who had lost her son; there, with a few gracious words, he comforted some deathly pale members of Hitler Youth whose father had died. So strong was the comfort the Führer gave to the bereaved that they no longer felt alone in their grief. Then, when the relatives raised their arms in salute and thanked Adolf Hitler once again in silence, Führer and people were so boundlessly close to one another in this hour of deepest affliction.

The Führer and the German people . . . Once there was a demonstration in the Frankfurt banquet hall and while the Führer was speaking inside to thousands of people, a woman stole up to his car and placed a very small bouquet of lilies of the valley—it was midwinter—on the seat in the car where she thought the Führer would be sitting. When the meeting was over, the motorcade began to move swiftly, but in the midst of the roaring cries of Heil Hitler, a very clear piercing voice was heard: "The lilies of the valley are from me!"

Hundreds and thousands of such touching and joyous, gripping and amusing stories could still be told. Yet they all say only one thing: "Here a miracle has taken place, something which happens only once in the history of a people: here Führer and People are one and the same, and the love that binds the people to their Führer is so great, so natural, so evident and so radiant, but it is also replete with strength.

What endless strength, what endless blessing it promises for both, for people and Führer, for the Führer and the German people!

November 9, 1934 in Munich. The Führer speaks in front of the Feldherrnhalle to listeners who have recently been admitted to the party from the Hitler Youth and the Union of German Girls.

The Führer as Orator

Dr. Joseph Goebbels

There are two kinds of orators who differ basically and essentially from one another. There are those who speak from the intellect and those who speak from the heart. Accordingly they are directed towards two kinds of men, those who listen with the intellect and those who listen with the heart. An intellect-speaker generally holds forth in parliament, while a heart-speaker has the people in mind.

If he wishes to speak effectively, the intellect-orator has above all to put together in order a great deal of statistics and knowledge. He has to master dialectics, just as the pianist must master his keyboard. With cool and inexorable logic he develops and assembles his thoughts and from them draws his inevitable conclusions. He focuses chiefly on people who cherish working with the intellect particularly or exclusively. Great and sweeping consequences remain denied to him. He does not understand how to motivate the masses in depth and to urge them on enthusiastically to goals that reach for the sky. He remains confined to pure didactics. Just as he himself is cold, he also leaves people cold. At best he may be persuasive, but he is never capable of mobilizing the masses and giving them the incentive to be unconcerned with their own self-interest or not to fear danger and death.

It is different with the orator who speaks from the heart. This is not to say that he has not mastered the skills the intellect-orator has mastered. Often, for him, these are merely tools which he, as a true virtuoso of the art of oratory, uses when required. Moreover, he has abilities that the intellect-orator will never have: with him clarity of diction is closely connected with the very obvious simplicity of the composition of his thought; he instinctively perceives what must be said and how it must be said. For him the extent of his use of poetical imagery is closely tied up with the monumental nature of the ideas. He is familiar with the secret inner workings of the soul of the masses and knows with a master's hand how to expose and reach them. His talks are declamatory works of art. With epic breadth he describes men and their situation; with a sharp stylus he inscribes his theses on the tablets of time; with high and noble pathos he builds high over his thought patterns the projecting pillar of his own world outlook. Just as his voice speaks from the depths of his race, so does he reach his hearers in the depths of their race. He makes the secret chords of the human soul ring out. He shakes up the sluggish and the lazy; he inspires the lukewarm and the questioning; he makes cowards into men and weaklings into heroes.

History hears such notes as these but rarely. Yet in this lethargic century they are urging with authority, and peoples and conditions are once again on the path to order.

These rhetorical men of genius are fate's drummers. They start out lonesomely in historical periods of collapse and abandonment and then suddenly and unexpectedly they rise up in the center of the brightest floodlights of a new stage of evolution. These are the orators who shape the history of peoples.

Like every great man, the orator has his own particular format and style. He can only speak as he is. For him his word is written on his very countenance. Whether he speaks in a proclamation, in a poster, in a letter and an idea, in an address or in a discourse, he always uses terms that suit his own being and nature.

In history there are many examples which incontestably verify the fact that great orators themselves resemble and equal what they do in greatness; the nature of their summons to the people and their call to people's hearts are fundamentally different, depending on the nature and character of the time. Caesar spoke differently to his legions than Frederick the Great did to his grenadiers; Napoleon spoke differently to his guards than Bismarck did to the political representatives of the Prussian Landtag. Each of them, however, used language that their hearers understood, and employed words and thoughts that caught fire in their minds and found an echo in their hearts. To the most profound and puzzling *daimon* of their time, they gave formative expression, and over the course of history they are known as the eternal heralds of the great ideas of the time—those ideas that made history and shaped people's lives.

It also seems that different races react to speeches differently, and it may be that the talents of some are too brittle for the art of effective persuasion, and that others are exactly fit and predestined for the task. It is not for nothing that we speak of Latin eloquence. The great profusion of these important rhetorical talents precisely among Romance peoples gives this expression a certain authenticity. And it follows from this fact that speaking talents used with regard to these people give them unlimited possibilities.

As for our own German people, the past has not been generous in this respect. We have had statesmen and soldiers, philosophers and scientists, musicians and poets, builders, and engineers, geniuses in planning and organization in food and shelter. But we have lacked any great oratorical talent. Since Fichte, with his classical oratory, captured the feeling of the German nation, there has been no one to warm the heart of the people, until Bismarck's challenge to his time. Once Bismarck was gone from the podium it was bereft of any real talent until, out of the collapse of the World War, there arose a new proclaimer of the people's misery. Between Bismarck and this man there was nothing but mediocrity, suited only for parliament or a council meeting. And it met only with icy reserve in the people themselves. This applies not only to oratory but to the time of history as well. There were no great ideas and no heaven-storming projects. The age foundered in an empty feeling of appeasement. The only apparent revolt against this was Marxism and it was secretly bound up with it. Its supporters were representatives of materialism and therefore unable to enkindle the sparks of true genius.

Revolutions, however, do give rise to genuine orators, and genuine orators make revolutions! The written or published word ought not to be underestimated, but the spoken word with its secret magic and its immediacy fans the senses and hearts of men into flame. It reaches the eyes and ears of masses of men, and through the sound of a human voice, they begin to understand, and even the wavering and doubting are irresistibly drawn into the voice's orbit.

Where would the statesmanly genius be, whom a higher and unfathomable fate first placed on the dark side of life, if he did not have the power of speech and the explosive might of the word at his disposal! This gives him the ability to make ideas

*The Führer with Reichsarbeitsführer Hierl in front of
47,000 workers on the Reich's Party Day in 1935.*

out of ideals and realities out of ideas. With his help men are rallied around his banner and ready to fight for him; urged on by him, men put health and life in the balance, in order to lead a new world to victory. Out of the propaganda of the word, the organization is formed, from the organization the Movement evolves, and the Movement wins over the State. Therefore, it is not only necessary for ideas to be correct; it is crucial that they be applied correctly to the masses and that the masses themselves become their bearers. Theories will always remain theories if living men do not put them into action. But in disturbing times,

living men only obey a call that catches fire in their hearts, since that call itself comes from the heart.

It is difficult to categorize the Führer as an orator. His skill in forming the masses is so singular and unique that it cannot be fitted into any schema or dogma. It would be absurd to think that he had ever attended a school of oratory or speech; he is a genius of the art of oratory, and this quality is completely indigenous, needing no outside help from anyone whatever. One can hardly maintain that the Führer once spoke differently from the way he now speaks, or that he ever could speak differently. He says what comes from his

Address to the staff of Blohm and Voss.

Taking charge of the Reichsführer School at Bernau in 1933.

heart, and therefore what goes immediately into the heart of the listener. He possesses the wonderful gift of instinctively perceiving what is in the air. He has the ability to express this so clearly, logically and limitlessly, that the listener will be transformed by what he hears, and his own views will be brought out. This is the essential secret of the magic of a Hitler speech. The Führer is neither exclusively a speaker from the intellect nor a speaker from the heart. He speaks from either point, depending on what the occasion demands. The essential characteristics of his manner of speaking are: structural clarity, relentless follow-through of an idea-sequence, simplicity and general comprehensibility of expression, razor-sharp dialectic, and a distinct and never misleading instinct for the masses and their feelings, a fascinating pathos that is applied with extreme economy, and the grace of an appeal to souls that never remains unanswered among the people.

Many years ago, when he was still far from a position of power, the Führer spoke at a meeting that was attended by a majority of his political opponents. From the outset he obviously met with an icy reception. In a two-hour fight with the obstinacy of his listeners, he dispelled all unresponsiveness and opposition, and at the end he was speaking to a bubbling sea of assent, jubilation and enthusiasm. When he had concluded, a man's voice shouted from the top of the balcony: "Hitler is Columbus!"

The essential of what he said was grasped. He had prepared the way for what was almost impossible. The times and the people's yearnings were intricate and mysterious, and yet he disentangled them and drew out their secrets. He showed them to his listeners again in simple and clear lines, so that the man in the street could at last perceive them, although he did not yet have the courage to express them. What everyone thought and felt, Hitler said! And that was not all. He had the courage of his convictions and against almost total opposition he drew out with purest logic the practical application of the conclusions which rose from the time itself and its demands.

The Führer is the first person in the evolution of Germany to use speech as a tool in order to make history. When he began, he had nothing like it. At the outset he was only supported by the power of his strong heart and the might of his pure word. With both he reached the innermost soul of the people. He did not speak like other people. Nor could he generally be likened to them. It was not as if he did not know the needs and sorrows which oppress the little man, or had not spoken of them; but with him they were only brush strokes on the horrible picture that he had painted of the collapse of Germany. He gave more than a bare description, he was no tendentious describer of backgrounds like the others. He brought out the

afflictions of the day in their general and national sense, and underlined their importance at the time. He appealed not to the bad but to the good instincts of the masses. His speech was a magnet that attracted what was left of the iron in the people's blood.

For a while stupid and overweaning bourgeois hollow-heads wanted to get rid of him as a "noise maker." They made themselves look ridiculous and did not know how to dispose of him. Since they themselves so completely lack the power of oratory, they consequently saw it as a minor art in building the state. They merely hankered after power without, however, realizing that Marxism had already taken the power away from them, and that under pressure they would hand it over to them once again. They set up a conventicle in which a people's movement was to be formed. They had a shot at armed uprisings in which a revolution was foreshadowed. They showed disdain for the masses when they could not become their masters. But the masses only bow to one who takes them under his inexorable command. They only obey when a person understands how to command. They have too fine an instinct not to be able to distinguish whether what is said is thought out or not.

This is evidence perhaps of the German people's inner incorruptibility, that it heard the call of a man who against state and society, against press and public opinion, against apparent reason and utility, relied solely on himself and his word. And, on the other hand, this again is evidence of the universal oratorical genius of the Führer, that his word alone caused a whole age to stop and think, overturned what appeared to be a stable state, and called for the birth of a new age.

A history-making oratorical figure, who lets loose such a process, must have all the possibilities of the spoken word at his disposal. This is the case with the Führer. He speaks to workers just as he, of course and especially, does to men of science. His word reaches deeply into the heart both of the farmer and the city-dweller. When he speaks to children, they feel that he speaks to them in their innermost selves. He speaks to men and the magic of his voice stirs up their innermost secret impulses. His addresses are historical philosophy, translated into the language of the people. He possesses the gift to lift great ages of the historical past out of their long oblivion, and he knows to whom he must show them, as something that they had known or perceived. It is completely wrong to confuse his words with that inciting tone of pseudo-learning that distinguishes the so-called discourses of learned heads.

His words always concentrate on thoughts of our race becoming a people and a nation. Thousands of statements in this regard are credited to him. Never has the listener heard such perceptive

The Führer at the election campaign for
Germany's freedom, March, 1936.

words. His words always emphasize to the masses the same great ideas of our pure German rebirth in ever-changing forms. Therefore, everything doctrinaire does harm to this variety of the art of speaking. A fact will be anticipated as an assertion, and then appears in the broader course of the statement in an inexhaustible profusion of examples. These examples will not be withdrawn from the realm of life and society at a determined level, so that the other levels of his power of demonstration may remain untouched. They are derived collectively from the life of the whole people which is rediscovering its own existence in them. They are extracted with such a strength of perception that the most blindly fanatical opponent ultimately capitulates in the knowledge that, in contrast to all the parliamentary word-jugglers, this speaker believes what he says.

Here everyday things take on new meaning and entrance every listener. Here the troubles of the times are sharply attacked not only with the steely tools of ideology, but also with wit and biting sarcasm. Here humor celebrates triumphs as it weeps with one eye and laughs with the other. Here we

*The Führer opens the 1935 Party Day of Freedom in
the historic Nuremberg Town Hall.*

find that note which also rings out in the sorrows and distresses of daily life.

An infallible indication of whether a given speech satisfies what is demanded of it is the fact that it not only sounds good but also reads well. The discourses of the Führer are stylistic masterpieces, whether he improvised them on the spur of the moment, worked them out from a few casual notes, or for meaningful international reasons he brings out a precisely fixed notion. If you are not in his immediate presence, you can scarcely tell whether he is speaking extemporaneously or from a carefully written text. Both are printable in the best sense of the term. The picture would not be complete if adequate mention were not made of the Führer as a superb builder and master of oratorical discussion. Publicity has been given to his controversy with the Social Democrats in the Reichstag in 1933, when he answered a clumsy and impertinent Jeremiad by the then Reichstag delegate Wels. The feeling was that it was a cat-and-mouse game. Marxism was forced from one corner to another. And where it hoped to find comfort it found only disappointment. With an

The orator

Adolf Hitler

almost breathtaking accuracy the oratorical lashes beat down on it. Without a manuscript, without notes, the Führer had his long-desired reckoning with the old hands of the Democratic parliament who were now receiving the death blow. How often had he driven them into a corner years before in his meetings, when they dared to confront him. At that time they were still able with their newspapers to lie about their feeble defeats and turn them into triumphant victories. Now they made him win out right before the eyes of the whole people in his authority, and here the débâcle was threatening them.

All those judges and public prosecutors knew how to sing a small song about this kind of inexorable, oratorical offensiveness. They wanted to lead Hitler as a defendant or witness onto slippery ice with their seemingly harmless and naïve questions or their dull and lusterless observations. Out of the People's Court proceedings of 1924, in which the rebellion of November 8–9, 1924, is juridically included, there would be a triumphant victory for the defendants, while the Führer confronted mountains of reports, malice and lack of comprehension, with the radiant power of his open veracity and the penetration of his over-

speaking to the youth   *on Reich's Party Day, 1935.*

powering eloquence. And not without regret, the Republic wanted to take cognizance of the outcome of the Leipzig 1930 German army and navy proceedings, which was supposed to demolish the Führer and his Movement. In reality, however, it was to become the springboard for an effective oratory that would influence the whole world. It is only with a shudder that we remember today the fact that a Jewish-Communist lawyer dared to put him up as a witness in a Berlin court for nine uninterrupted hours with rapid-fire questions. And we recall with proud satisfaction that Jewish Bolshevism was confronted by an opponent who

upset its calculations and would not relent until it lay overcome on the ground.

We saw and witnessed the Führer as an orator on the Party Day of Freedom in 1935. In the space of seven days he spoke to the masses fifteen times. Not a single time were the same thoughts brought forth or were the same turns of phrase used. Everything was always new and fresh, vital and penetrating. He spoke differently to the administrators than he did to the Storm Troopers and the SS men, differently to the youth than to the women. He, who in his great cultural oratory revealed the most secret secrets of artistic creation, spoke in his address to the Wehrmacht to the last soldier in the last battalion and would be understood by him. Here is the span of a bow, under which the life of the whole German people moves and runs its course. He has become an announcer of the word, approaching the thousandfold existence with the divine grace of oratory.

However, the Führer is the greatest as an orator when he speaks to a small group. Here he carries on a continual exchange with each individual listener. Time moves rapidly and the constant flow of thoughts awakens in the listener an interest that never tires, and is constantly renewed. Either he speaks accidentally on a theme connected with a special branch of science, which surprises everybody, even the specialist, or else he talks about things mentioned incidentally by someone and puts them in their proper perspective.

Here the Führer goes deeply and in detail, as much as a public speech allows, into the kernel of things, so that he can demonstrate them with inexorable logic. Only someone who has listened to him on a one-to-one basis could grasp the whole greatness of his oratorical genius.

Actually, we can say of his addresses to the people and to the world that they are words that find an audience that history has never seen before.

But they are also words that catch fire in people's hearts and without interruption they work toward the formation of a new international age. Today in the whole civilized world there is hardly a man who has not at least once heard the sound of his voice, and whether he understood his words or not, from the magic of their tone he felt he was spoken to in his innermost heart. Our people can feel lucky to know that there is a voice over them on which the world eavesdrops, a blessed voice that forms thoughts from words, and with these thoughts sets a new age in motion. This man listens to those people who have the courage to say yes and no, without the falsifying "if" or "but" of a subordinate clause. In a situation where in all the countries of the earth millions and millions of men are stricken with the bitterest sorrow, sorest affliction, and most frightful need, where hardly a star shines through the dark clouds that cover Europe's sky, where peoples are filled with and driven by unclear yearnings which they do not have the gift or the grace to express, there stands over Germany, one man among the untold millions, to whom, when man grows dumb in his torment, a God gave the ability to say what we suffer!

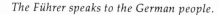

The Führer speaks to the German people.

A walk in the Obersalzberg.

The Führer in His Private Life

Obergruppenführer Wilhelm Brückner

It is obvious that a man who is so occupied with political work as is the Führer must sacrifice his private life. And when he wants to free himself from the pressure of his duties, the problems of politics still follow him even into the furthest corner of the German homeland, whether it is a small quiet village on the dunes of the Baltic or Wachenfeld House in the Obersalzberg. They hasten to him in the form of phone calls and telegrams, letters and reports, and he cannot banish from his heart the never-ceasing political work which is his deep concern for Germany. With this concern the Führer retires late at night, and with the same concern he wakes up early in the morning. He is pursued by problems of foreign affairs, the urgencies of the new work program, difficulties coming from the area of political finance, the need to assure enough food for the nourishment of the German people, problems of the education of the youth, questions of German culture, decisions within the framework of the recovery of German military security . . . And so it goes, on and on. There is hardly a conversation that does not lead into the midst of the most central political

On the Obersalzberg. A neighbor greets the Führer.

He may look through the telescope.

Prime Minister Göring with the Führer on the Obersalzberg.

A meeting on the Obersalzberg.

Wachenfeld House on the Obersalzberg near Berchtesgaden.

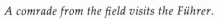

A comrade from the field visits the Führer.

A walk in the mountains.

Days of calm. The Führer with little Helga Goebbels.

questions, nor an occurrence that does not immediately call for most important decisions. Everything in Germany really begins and ends with this man. And when he takes a few days of complete rest in seclusion, it is only to prepare for great new decisions, for a new, intensive work-achievement program. Yes, the telegrams from his directors and ministers also reach him by airplane.

Thus, the Führer's private life is absorbed in his official duties, in his work for Germany, and when we want to speak of his private life, we can only say that it is only present insofar as he transfers his political work from his office in the Chancellery to smaller official spaces.

In addition, he finds time to deal with all the questions of art and science. His greatest and most beautiful form of recreation, after a grinding day's work, is found in music, in listening to an opera or a symphonic concert. He is completely detached from the pressing questions of the day, and then many a great creative thought rises out of his reverie, within the mighty realm of sound.

Also, from time to time, in the rooms of his official residence in the Chancellery, the Führer has leading German artists as guests. To him they bring the best creations of our time, and often after the artistic recitals, conversations on music and drama, poetry and the novel, architecture and philosophy go on until late into the night. After such an evening hardly anyone leaves the house without being filled with valued inspirations.

In addition to music, the theater and architecture, the Führer is especially interested in the cinema, since it is the youngest branch of artistic production. A projector in the great hall of the Chancellery makes it possible, in between the pressing questions of the day, for him to view productions from Germany and the world over. The film makers were also given many new stimuli by the Führer out of his own knowledge.

Often the Führer invites visitors, who have come on official business, to have lunch with him. This way he can find the time to deal with some questions that especially struck him during the official meeting, and to delve into them more fully. His guests then will come from different areas of work and interest, officers and scientists, economists and men of the arts, high Party leaders and old comrades from the war and the early days of the Movement. At lunch with the Führer, they

Potluck. Also at the Chancellor's.

receive new knowledge and stimuli, not only from him but also from one another during the course of the conversation.

The Führer happily uses the weekend personally to satisfy himself about the mood of the people, and also to get an idea for himself about the advancement made in construction work, without officially announced inspections. Then he motors with his old and valued car from combat days through the provinces of Germany. In almost every place there are some memories at least from the time of the struggle for power. For his staff, it is always a new and profound experience to see the great love the people show for the Führer on these trips.

There are some places in Germany to which the Führer is always especially glad to return for a shorter rest. Most especially it is that house in the Obersalzberg—so well known to all Germans— which is so closely bound up with the history of the Movement. On the Baltic and North Seas there are also a few places hidden away in the dunes which the Führer likes to search out for a short rest or to prepare for especially important conferences. Walks through the beechwoods at sunset

on the sea beach often provide the needed rest, and at the same time produce important political decisions. Without shyness, children come up to the Führer on such walks, give him their hands, chat with him and tell him all their little experiences which for them are so important. Then it may happen that the Führer, as in the most important conversations, participates for a few minutes in the joys and sorrows of one of these children.

In one of the larger harbors, the navy gathered around the Führer and a short informal evening was animated by war tales, accounts of U-boat trips and of the battle of Jutland. The same thing happens in the small garrisons out in the country, where the Führer himself will often tell thrilling and impressive stories of his own war experiences on the Western Front.

On his trips he often stops at especially charming points in the countryside for a short picnic, either on a glorious sunny day in summer or in the warm and beautiful moonlight. It frequently happens that berry-pickers and wood-gatherers suddenly appear and are surprised when they realize that it is the Führer who, here in a woodland

Good news.

glade, was peeling an apple or eating some bread. Then he makes a sign to those who were hesitant and invites them to take part in the meal.

Many people wonder why the Führer chose the Obersalzberg for his home. But whoever has been there understands that in all Germany there is hardly any place where in addition to the majestic mountains one has such a far-reaching view of the beauties of the world. To the North, in an area between the mountains, at the foot of the Gaisberg, there lies the old episcopal city of Salzburg. On sultry days one can see the fortress and the little town with the naked eye. With a telescope, without the warm wind which tends to bring things closer, all the details of the buildings can be recognized. To the left, from the Obersalzberg looms up the massif of the Untersberg, whose changing and impressive colors provide a new experience daily. When one looks still further to the left, one can see the Watzmann and the mountain channels around it, curving far behind the Obersalzberg and culminating in the Hohe Göll.

Here no day is like any other. At times the morning haze wages a desperate battle with the rising sun until it is dispelled, rising up from the valleys, and ends up at noon as light white clouds in the azure-blue sky. At other times, the day begins with bright sunshine and everything is clear and distinct down to the last detail. The warm wind comes down from the heights and fills the valleys round about with its mild and ardent mood. Then again the mountains are pelted with rain and snow storms and the wind rushes around the simple little country house.

Here in the midst of nature's splendor, symbolic of what is happening to man, lives the Führer. He works out his great discourses, which have already given a new jolt or a new direction not only to the situation in Germany but to the politics of the world as well. Here take place the decisive discussions that give a definitive form to statutes that have been worked out over the centuries.

A German American from the Steuben Company grasped the meaning and importance of this little country house, which he got to know on a visit to his homeland, and later said something like the following: "We Germans from America have not known the new Germany. We knew only the old Germany and we saw it again in the new as we visited the palaces and castles of earlier

*A Wolf Cub hands the Führer a letter
from his sick mother.*

A little visit to the Führer on the Obersalzberg.

times. Now, however, we have come to know this house and in it have experienced an obvious example of the contrast between the Germany created by Adolf Hitler and the old. We now also know what an inexhaustible fountain it is from which he creates the substance for his oratory."

And it is true that here, far from the tangle and bustle of everyday life, the seeking mind, led on by the unshakeable greatness of the landscape, discovers the correct paths for people and fatherland. However, the Führer cannot enjoy this wonderful beauty of nature like a tourist on holiday who has left all his business behind. From the moment he arrives at the Obersalzberg, he finds an impressive number of letters and reports, telegrams and telephone messages, and with every mailman come new bundles of work. The ministers and government officials call almost every day in order to get the Führer's opinion on some important and pressing concern. Often they come themselves to Berchtesgaden to talk with the Führer during his short period of rest. Party questions, which in Berlin must be pushed into the background in the face of important political judgments, are solved here and many books of esthetic

and political literature from Germany and abroad, which lay forgotten in the Chancery waiting to be read, will be thoroughly studied here by the Führer in peace and quiet. The light in his room burns until late at night. His staff has already long since gone to sleep, a marvelous deep quiet reigns, and the Führer reads. These are his happy hours. On another morning, however, the telephone trunk exchange advises that there have already been dozens of advance calls, reports are again ready, and the mail has piled up. It is always the case: when the Führer goes "for a rest" to the Obersalzberg, the mail and phone services in Berchtesgaden are intensely active. And those who surround the Führer also have their full measure of work; then thoughts again bear fruit and decisions swiftly mature.

Before the common breakfast, the Führer has already read the newspapers. He goes through them himself, and does not allow prepared excerpts. Then his adjutants, his press chief and the rest of the men on his staff come and give a short report about what is on for the day. Once breakfast is over, there is the immediate arrival of the announced visitors, government officials, minis-

On the G'schwandner pastureland, near Garmisch.

*The Führer during the summer vacation near Berchtesgaden
where Dietrich Eckart lived for a long time.*

An evening in the Obersalzberg.

"Here, my Führer, is my grandchild."

The happiness of motherhood.

Wolf Cubs with the Führer.

The Führer in front of his villa in the Obersalzberg.

ters, close collaborators and party comrades. In the meanwhile the mail was prepared and brought to the Führer, who either sketches out a short reply or dictates an answer in full. The morning goes by quickly.

Most welcome guests at the Obersalzberg are always the old comrades in arms: Party Member Göring, Party Member Dr. Goebbels, the Minister of the Exchequer Schwarz, Minister Adolf Wagner, as well as the Minister of War and many others.

The work-filled morning is followed by a shorter or longer midday walk, or a drive around the neighborhood. The Führer is especially happy to go in summer or winter to the "Göll-Häusl" where Dietrich Eckart once lived until death snatched him from the Führer's side.

The Führer is equally happy to drive over to the Königsee, that jewel of the German mountain landscape, where the perpendicular slope of the Watzmann and the Idyll of Bartholomae always impress one with their unforgettable splendor.

Time does not allow for longer walks and after the noon meal work has to be continued. This lasts until coffee time, when a short space of time is taken out to go over to the little mountain inn on

the Hochlenzer, or to pay a visit to the house of Prime Minister Göring when the master of the house is there. Then Party Member Göring is happy to extend an invitation to an archery match, at which he excels.

Often, however, the Führer only has just barely enough time left in the day to spend in the garden of his house with his Alsatian wolfhounds, who idolize him, or else in winter to pensively watch the birds perched on the many feeders, and enjoying what Adolf Hitler had put out for them in the morning. Thus the day's program changes from morning to morning. Only one thing never changes. Every day hundreds and thousands of his fellow countrymen assemble below on the high road in order to see the Führer at noon. The Führer well knows that they have all come to Berchtesgaden not only to see him, but to express to him the love of the whole German people, and he lets nothing stand in the way of their fulfilling their ardent wish. Each time it is a deeply moving picture to experience the exultation which breaks out when the Führer goes down and walks among them. Workers of brow and fist are come together from every part of Germany, and every time it is like a pilgrimage. They all, whether big or small,

On the Obersee near Berchtesgaden.

pass by the Führer. Their eyes shine, their hands are raised in greeting, and many of them have tears in their eyes from the emotion of the moment. From the rows of the passers-by resound the acclamations which proclaim the kinship of all members in one single German family: "From Upper Silesia . . . From East Prussia . . . From Schleswig . . . From Oldenburg . . . From Saxony . . . From Hamburg . . ." etc. Little Wolf Cubs and B.D.M. girls do not remain in the background. Nimble as weasels, they run to the Führer and present him with carefully prepared bouquets of flowers. They are happy when the Führer converses with them, but still happier when he invites some of them to lunch or coffee.

At mealtimes all his guests and his assistants sit light-heartedly together and often peals of laughter are heard in the room. These short minutes are spent in relaxation and calm. Many architects and artists come for a visit and show the Führer their latest plans. The Führer is pleased with everything in the new race-culture build-up and he discusses at length the plans they show him. Also Dr. Todt, the inspector general of highways, receives the Führer's full attention for his plans and photographs. The old comrades-in-arms of the Führer from the time of the World War are also always welcome guests at the Obersalzberg.

When, however, work at the Obersalzberg does not allow for a real break, the Führer takes short and energetic walks which give him new vigor; it does not matter to him whether the summer sun beats down from the sky, or crunching snow covers the mountains, whether rain is pouring down, or the fog is blocking visibility. These walks are not always an unmixed joy for the Führer's staff, who learned mountain-climbing in the big city, since the Führer walks very rapidly and without stopping, and it is often hard even for trained people to keep up with him. Thus his adjutants frequently have trouble in holding the pace till the end. While they are already panting hard, the Führer is still striding on fearlessly and tirelessly.

As short as these vacation days are, they generally become even shorter on account of unexpected events. But one thing is certain: nowhere else can the Führer find such a pleasant respite in his hectic life than he can here in the mountains.

Just as the mountains have remained perpetually there throughout the millennia, so will the Führer's work, begun here, continue perpetually over the millennia in his people.

Summer vacation on the Obersalzberg.

Diplomatic reception. New Year's, 1934.

The Führer as Statesman

DR. JOSEPH GOEBBELS

All human greatness has its source in race. Instinct is its signpost and intuition its great grace. It is only with qualifications that the intellect is given a share in the works of true genius; it is more concerned with giving them meaning and direction and with showing them to later observers. These precepts are most important for this art, this highest and most noble activity of men, which brings them closer to their divine origin. They are similarly valuable and meaningful in the area of major politics. It is not for no reason that we call politics the art of statesmanship. It is indeed an art, since it has all the essential features of artistic creativity. The sculptor puts chisel and hammer to submissive stone so as to blow divine breath into it. What was raw marble becomes artistic form. The painter uses the primary matter of color so that he can create noble pictures from nature, and to a certain degree give form to nature a second time. The poet puts phrases together,

which by themselves would be formless sounds, and creates a poem, a drama or an epic performance in which he modifies the human passions of good and evil.

The statesman has the raw material of the masses at his disposal. With the power of his word and work he kneads them into living and breathing people. His great and ingenious projects make the people the nation's objective. The people are formed into a homogeneity by genius, which is the inspiration that becomes the true artist's instrument. In all these areas there are artisans who are present and who can differentiate their problems and obligations. With diligence and industry learn their business, and they are qualified if they belong to the better part of their profession, which is a valuable and comprehensive special branch of science, and of which they have an appropriate understanding. Yet for them, what they do is a profession and not an avocation or a job. They are the talents of artistic activity. But the real artist works like a genius.

It is here that talent differs from genius; talent creates out of practical experience, out of learning, and perhaps also out of a fantasy-filled intellect, but genius creates from grace. It works to bring about a higher order and with it fulfills the precept which it closely follows. Geniuses overthrow worlds and build new ones. They are the great signposts of the peoples. After them the times become coordinated. They put aright the weak in whom history takes its course.

The saying that the child is hidden in every man is especially true of the genius. The genius behaves and operates out of childlike simplicity, and stands up to things with a self-assurance and a lack of self-consciousness that are customarily the prerogatives of children.

The ingenious statesman dares the impossible in order to make the possible possible. His essential strength is in the simplification of seemingly insoluble complications. Before the average intellect has seen or known a solution to impatiently anticipated problems, our great Führer is already involved in solving them.

There was an urgent problem with which we Germans were faced after the War. It was this: how to form a nation that thinks, feels and negotiates uniformly, out of such a conglomerate of regions, parties, organizations and individuals. The problem, however, did not originate through the War, but the confusion it perpetrated finally caused us to lose the War. As a result of its inner conflicts, for many years Germany remained cut off from the world political scene. We Germans had inner divergences of views of a religious, economic or social nature, that were distributed throughout the land. While these differences kept us apart, other nations who had already become aware of their own world-political destiny took possession of the world.

But first the War had made manifest the broader impossibility of this situation. Without learning from this frightful model, the Germans did exactly the opposite of what history demanded of them. Never before in Germany had particularism of every kind celebrated such orgies as at this period, when we were most strongly aware of our inner determination.

In the years after the War there was frequently the impression that Germany relinquished the field of the interplay of the great world powers, and withdrew into provincial isolation. There was little support for a common national way of thinking, and the Weimar situation represented to a certain degree the perpetuation of inner unrest whose beneficiaries were the parliamentary parties. Their state ran from this problem because their vigilance was directed more inwardly than outwardly. Their goal was to maintain and pre-

serve what little we had left internally, such as the freedom to travel where we liked, and our external sovereignty.

A statesmanly genius appearing at this time would experience his first and most difficult trial, when he recognized the apparent hopelessness of the battle that raged within the State itself to restore the worldwide importance of Germany. There seemed hardly any reason even to continue it. Through the signing of the Versailles treaty the State had surrendered this worldwide importance for all time. In addition, it jealously observed the terms of this document and every impulse of national feeling was looked upon as an assault on the very existence of the State and punished as such.

We must therefore look for the true statesman not within the Party or the State, but outside of both. The State itself had to fall so that the process of the moral, social and economic restoration of the German people could make it possible to create a state that would be genuine and appropriate to its nature. In the battle against the State, a state within the State would be built. On this new State all the laws must be tested for their practicality and their susceptibility to organization, and they then would become the laws of the new State. The point was not merely to set in opposition to the Weimar theory simply another new theory, but rather to produce something fully thought out and properly directed. Around this new theory there should be an association of men who would give life, color and real existence to it. Within the Weimar non-State there had to be set up an opposition state which would produce a people within the people as well. Only in accordance with these principles could the new formation-process of the German Nation be initiated.

This was the beginning of the Führer's statesmanship.

Beforehand, we must clarify some fundamental decisions that to a certain degree had become the essential source of his whole political action program. As an unknown lance corporal in the World War, in the confusion of a revolution, he spoke as a construction officer to the Bavarian garrisons. There he made a series of resolutions which terminated in the absolutely sure and sovereign instinct of statesmanly genius. Although these were understood by practically no one, they later became the essential cause of his fabulous and fantastic rise, producing the corroboration of the accuracy of the world picture which he had in his mind. He could easily have joined one of the existing parties. This would have meant a quiet and secure life for him with all sorts of possibilities for ascent. He might have been able to appease his agonized conscience by the fact that one should be saving what still could be saved and therefore choose the lesser evil. He did nothing of the kind.

A visitor to the Chancellery (Prime Minister Gömbös).

And this was because none of the existing parties had either the possibility or the guarantee of putting an end to the internal strife in Germany. His aim was to bring the Germans together and to solve the national German problem in a statesmanly sense. Here there is already the emergence of a man instinctively blessed, who rather than encumbering his work with a compromise at the outset, took on himself a seemingly hopeless battle against State, Money, Press and Parties.

At that time it was the fashion to go along with the State. Two positions then were possible: identifying with the State or having to and being able to reform it from within. The Führer chose neither position. He knew that this State was not fulfilling its purpose, that it could not be transformed but rather should be eliminated so as to make it possible to build a true State. There were both men and parties who saw or pretended to see the impossibility of reforming the Weimar system from within, and therefore took a stand against it. But they were encumbered from the outset with the compromise of concluding at least a temporary peace with the Weimar Democracy. Only the Führer could say, from the first to the last day of his opposition, that he never made a pact with the parliamentary regime and as it happened, in the last hour, it was he who gave it the death blow.

A historic encounter. Eden and Simon with the Führer.

The German cabinet at the proclamation of the regulations for national defense.

After the New Year's diplomatic reception in 1936.

The Führer and Foreign Minister von Neurath.

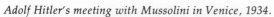

Adolf Hitler's meeting with Mussolini in Venice, 1934.

In the Chancellery:
the Führer and his Chief of Staff, Lutze.

*The chancellor at the New Year's reception, talking with
François-Poncet, the French ambassador.*

In the Chancellery.

The Führer and the Polish Foreign Minister Beck.

English sympathizers with the Führer.

New Year's reception, 1935. The Führer speaks with the dean of the diplomatic corps.

The German Press Chief, Dr. Dietrich, submits press releases to the Führer.

National Day of Mourning, 1934.
The Ceremony at the Berlin State Opera house.

Parties and men at this time never spoke to the people as a people; they directed themselves always only to particular elements within the people. The labor parties spoke to the workers, the bourgeois parties to the bourgeoisie, the confessional parties to their particular religious groups, and the peasant parties to the peasantry. In the first assemblies of the National Socialist Workers Party in Munich, at which the Führer could count on barely one hundred men, to the superficial observer it may have seemed absurd that the call went out to the people as a whole. They spoke neither to the educated nor the proletariat, and they had the courage to say the unpopular and refused to buy the approbation of the masses through cheap flattery. We have to go back to this early period of the National Socialist Movement and to the origin of the essential leadership of Adolf Hitler in order to understand the miracle of his statesmanship, which is grounded in these early days. It was not the times that changed the Führer, the Führer changed the times. What at that time seemed to be a paradox has long since become self-evident. And indeed, it would not be

The Führer in front of the Imperial Palace at Goslar, on the occasion of the Harvest Thanksgiving Festival, 1934.

self-evident of itself; it needed a clear and uncompromising decision by one man and a tough and relentless battle for it to succeed.

It would have been easy then to posit certain extravagant social demands which would have further set the Führer and his Movement apart from its real purpose. It can also be granted that for the first few years it might have been more comfortable to have been a supporter of these social demands. The Führer did not do this. He formed an ideological platform for his Movement, which to a certain degree became the directive foundation of his Party and his State. The essential distinguishing mark of this world ideology was the combining of the national and socialist principles. For the highest echelons as well as for the man in the street these were understandably the real motivating forces of the time, although they remained in a bitter feud with one another. Yet on an extended basis they came to be joined together. The fact that nothing needed to be changed, neither in the program or the world ideology, neither the flag or the name of the National Socialist Movement, when it came to power is proof of how far-sighted and statesmanly was the foundation of National Socialism even in the very beginning. The Führer decided that the Movement would make no compromises and would combine the sternest intransigence in what is basic with the greatest elasticity in methodical concerted action. From the outset it waged a life-and-death struggle with parliamentarianism until it was destroyed. It diverted the terror of the Marxist parties not with craven and cowardly phrases but by setting power against power. If its first brave surprise attack to secure power (No-vember 8–9, 1923) was a failure, later historians have examined it and found what was attained and also what was prevented. And it can be said today that the Führer's behavior was abundantly justified. How did these bourgeois politicians from the time of the Republic behave after the failed Putsch? They either fled abroad or else were not present at all. With the Führer it was quite different! He stood at the head of his men, was the first among the defendants, walked on no special golden bridge built for him by the court or the government, made no protest, confessed openly

Foreign military attachés at the Party Day in Nuremberg.

that he had wanted to overthrow the state and that he would do so again when he had the opportunity. He did what for the moment seemed to be the most dangerous and most destructive thing possible, but by doing so he saved the Movement and his own work. The command he had over the great trial in the Munich people's court is a statesmanly act of utmost importance. He knows all elements of political behavior in the best sense of the term. Here daring is paired with logic, openness with courage, contempt for danger with extreme effort. It was a last dice game where everything was won since everything was ventured. His defense of himself against the non-State of Versailles and Weimar raised up thousands and millions of people who until then had only dreamed of or longed for what he did, and it swept them up in a current of enthusiastic admiration.

The Führer cannot be made accountable for the path taken by the Party during his imprisonment. He clearly recognized the problems of statesmanship which were his and the Party's after his release. This proved the fact that he permitted no attempts at agreements with the so-called parlia-

A meeting of German governors in the Chancellery presided over by the Führer.

The Führer receives a Japanese Navy delegation in 1934.

National Labor Day, 1934. Youth demonstration in the Berlin Lustgarten on May 1.
The Führer's departure after his great speech to the youth.

mentarians, but rather refounded the old Movement in accordance with its original principles. A difficult, sacrificial and disciplined battle over the renewed importance of the Party began. For a year it seemed that the undertaking was hopeless. At this time the National Socialist German Workers Party was held in low esteem and it was well aware of the hatred of its opponents. Although it was not apparent from the outside, there was an inner development of a fruitful organic process of gradually rebuilding the Movement and its individual organizations. If someone would want to form an opinion about a statesman's manner of gathering people with specific characteristics and temperaments about him and his work, the Führer has no need to fear this judgment. Very seldom has an historical age seen such a plethora of genuinely efficient people such as ours. It is easy to establish their presence today. However, it was difficult to seek them out from the broad mass of supporters, to recognize their gifts instinctively, and to point out their capabilities corresponding to their positions in the Movement's struggle and later within the State itself.

In 1928 there were only twelve delegates from the National Socialist Movement in parliament, while in two years their number increased almost tenfold. The Party was again in the limelight and therefore faced with its decisive test. It knew how up until now all other parties had been mollified by being given a few unimportant ministerial posts and thus having a rôle to play in the Regime. The Party also knew, however, that once the battle was begun it would be carried on no matter what until the end, with the slogan: "All or Nothing."

Again the Führer's statesmanly instinct found the correct decision. The battle went on and during the Army-Navy trial before the Leipzig State court it found its special note in the proclamation of the legality viewpoint by the Führer himself. At the beginning of this trial, no one in the regime had any inkling of what a Berlin Democratic newspaper ascertained at its conclusion, namely that Adolf Hitler was the essential winner, and in addition that the highest German court gave him the possibility before the jury in the presence of the whole world to solidify his legality principle under oath. No concessions were made to his own

May 1 at Tempelhof Field.

The gradual scuttling and systematic mollification of the bourgeois parties was the next goal. experiences, but he could rely on this continually in the continuation of his battle against the Republic. Here was the decisive point, and even here the Führer is set apart from his adversaries in that he recognized with statesmanly vision the possibilities of this trial at its beginning and not, as his opponents did, at its end. He was obviously very clear about the fact that he had to uphold the principle of legality against the extremists in his own party, but he also knew that this was necessary if the Movement in general were to be involved.

Two years later, after tireless efforts, it managed to bring down the Brüning government. The apparent tolerance vis-à-vis the von Papen government led up to August 13, 1932, and here again the great hour for a real statesman had come. Should one be satisfied with half or want everything? Every artisan of politics would have picked the first alternative. Thousands of examples out of Germany's past attest to this. Yet, as a true statesman, the Führer decided on the second. He was repaid for his great and daring decision with two million votes in the 1932 November election. With a till then unused concentration of all his strength, he made one last assault against the regime in the

Lippe election campaign in the beginning of January, 1933. Two weeks later he took power.

The bond between Hindenburg and Hitler was the first symbol of this synthesis. Here tradition and revolution joined hands. The statesmanly genius of the Führer wrought the miracle, reconciling with the real forces of tradition a supreme revolution that was brought about without the shedding of blood.

Here we see preserved the intuition-sure instinct of a man in complete control, who is brought to fulfillment by an inner law. Here seemingly radical statements that were derided brought about a magnificent revolution. A world was overthrown and a new world built up.

The miracle of German unification was what followed. If on March 21, 1933, the Führer brought the tradition-bound forces into the government, on May 1, 1933, he led the German worker-caste into it as well. The occupation of the Trade Union buildings at the tactically correct and only possible moment was an almost direct consequence of this process of unifying the people. The setting up of a four-year plan for the solving of the most pressing problems of German life was a far-sighted and far-reaching projection which allowed enough time so that it could be worked out calmly and without nervousness. During the following period acute problems caused some confusion in government politics. The Führer brought out a few small but decisive ones and they were solved expediently. In the best sense of the word, he acted as a statesman. Never was there a revolutionary of such importance so far removed from hysteria and temerity as he. Never has there been a political figure who made history who worked so clearly and resolutely, without haste and uproar, as he. And where in history has such a miracle been wrought in the face of foreign political pressure as here?

Courage and daring were the sponsors of the Führer's resolution to get Germany out of the League of Nations. What would have filled the faint-hearted with despair was done here with superior assurance, since it was necessary and had to be risked. The greatest resolution of the first year was indeed statesmanly when he gave the vote to the people. It was statesmanly too when he proclaimed German military freedom at the decisive hour and brought this to the attention of the world at large, with the conviction that the time was right and that people had to act accordingly. His real vocation proved itself here. And here he works out of an inspiration that is not from the intellect but from the race.

Now we have a German people who are again in a position to protect their national life on their own. Through an honorable agreement with England they have established a Navy worthy of their nationhood. They walk again today in the orbit of other peoples as a great power. To an increasing extent they excite the admiration or at least the envy of the whole world. They are more and more visible as the most important element in world peace. And all of this is the result of a statesmanly evolution from the seven-man party in Munich to the Great Power status of the German Reich. There are a number of decisions included in this evolution. All together they produce a picture of a fabulous and fantastic rise which will be exalted by later historians unquestionably as the greatest political miracle of the 20th century. Here one gets the unerring feeling of what is possible in a twinkling of an eye and what is not possible. Here are bound together clarity in leadership and clear-sighted action. Here in depth an untainted political instinct was obtained, and a miracle was wrought since he believed in miracles.

Today Germany harbors a people quite different from that of years ago. It owes its strength and belief to the sure and unerring leadership of a true statesman who not only knows what he wants, but wants what he knows. He is one of history's predestined. Therefore, he is great enough to be simple, and simple enough to be great.

The Führer laying the foundation wall of the Assembly Building in Adolf-Hitler Koog.

The Führer and the German Worker

Dr. Robert Ley

Since the victory of National Socialism, the German people's way of life has been plainly marked by the position of the worker in the new German State and the value placed on both the worker and his work.

The proletariat became a class at the moment that Liberalism began to command the thinking world of Europe. Liberalism saw work as something distasteful, almost as something dishonorable. Its highest ideal was to be able to live off the work of others. No longer was the goal that many sought after working together to build the future of one's own people with a sense of joy; it had

become rather to pass through as quickly as possible the distasteful stage of work in order to live as men of private means, coupon holders who make money from other's work and from commissions. Obviously, such a view of life must involve a gradation of work and we can give some idea of their notion: at the very top there is the idleness of the blasé, then the work of tradesmen in gold or commodities, the intellectual work, and finally manual labor.

Manual labor, by God, was the filthiest and most degrading thing that could happen to a man. Whoever had the misfortune to earn his living by

With the workers in Siemenstadt.

working with his own hands was already fully degraded and excluded from "better society." He was "impossible." The depth to which this Liberal outlook poisoned healthy people's perception is alone proof of the fact that even the worker himself, toiling with his body day after day, looked upon himself as a déclassé person. He scraped together all his pennies in order to have his son become "something better," possibly a craftsman. Every penny of his meager salary he put toward this goal so he could send his son to the *Gymnasium,* [Classical High School] or at least to the *Oberrealschule,* [Trade School] if the son happened to find Latin and Greek so difficult. And the father himself said that this should happen not only so his son might have life easier or that he would be better prepared, or in a word, better off than his father, but so that he might *be better* than his father.

Do we understand the whole madness of this thinking? It is a madness that would again be systematically supported by Marxism. The inferiority complex already produced in the German working man by Liberal arrogance was deepened and the worker was inoculated with the feeling that he was a "disinherited person," and even a "prole-tarian." Consequently, his hatred for the "better people" was validated.

What an accursed crime was committed by the root power of Liberalism and Marxism with their caste-and-class spirit and their class hatred!

Under Marxist leadership the worker believed he could better his situation by refusing to work. Under Liberal stupefaction wide circles of "refined people" would go hungry rather than look for honest work. The real German principle: "Work does not defile" became turned into its opposite: "Work defiles"! The propertied people, the "haves," looked upon the workers as slaves. The worker avenged himself and looked upon those who gave out jobs as parasites and drones, and then proceeded to act accordingly. Both sides, however, generally did not realize that their attitude and resultant actions would have in a short time destroyed the people of which, for better or worse, they were a part. No one had any concept of a fatherland called Germany, no matter what group they belonged to.

It is at this point that Adolf Hitler's unprecedented work began. He recognized that he himself could not deal either with the "haves" or the "have-nots," nor with the employers nor with the employees, and that Marxism was not to be up-rooted without the extermination of arrogant and reactionary Liberalism. What he did was to place a completely new and therefore very old sense of worth in the people themselves. His short and clear sentences got the people to sit up and listen. First a few were deeply moved, then more and more and finally all realized that for a hundred years they had been wandering about in a dark and most dreadful night. The scales fell from their eyes and a new bright understanding came over them. In the light of this understanding, it became evident that everything that up to now had been a cause of hostility among them as an unreconcilable antithesis was actually nothing more than a mortal enmity directed toward an unsubstantial nothing. The Führer taught: You are nothing, your people is everything. When you work you work for the people. Consequently work is an honor. There is no partiality or distinction in work. The work of a General Manager has no more inner worth and is no better than the work of a street sweeper. It does not depend on what kind of work, but rather on how that work is done. Whoever does not work loses honor in the people's community. Work does not defile. It ennobles, regardless of whether the work is done with the mind or the fist. Only existing as a drone brings dishonor as well as the disdain of a working fellow-countryman.

And these phrases do not remain mere theory. In 1933 the German worker had been seduced by Marxism to some extent and both he and the reactionary and stupid Liberals were skeptical. They believed that National Socialism was not all that earnest in its world outlook. Yet in the shortest time this opinion was changed and today the German worker is the most stalwart follower of the Führer. He redeemed him from a proletarian existence, and restored honor to him and to work itself since Liberalism and Marxism had taken it away, Finally, he gave him the ability to be what in the innermost reaches of his soul he had always fought for, a man respected among men, a man whose work was highly valued. Now the only differentiation that existed was in the area of accomplishment and ability.

Proof of this is that the German workers follow the Führer enthusiastically. They stand solidly man for man next to the First Worker of the Reich. Now the Liberal Party of the "haves" has learned about National Socialist thinking, and in the third year of the National Socialist Reich they now know this new ethic of work in its external expression with the establishment of the German Work-Front as an organization which includes all creative Germans, from the general manager to the apprentice. From this day on in Germany there are only German working men and German operations. With this the past is finally dead. The aristocracy of work rules in Germany.

However, this could only have been done if each member of the German people learned a new way of thinking and began to look at the world in a new way, namely through National Socialism.

The Führer once said: "Whoever wants to be a true Socialist must first have experienced misery physically, in his own body." The German working masses know that for many years the Führer himself was a manual laborer and experienced in his own body the pains and sufferings involved in working from morning to night in rain, wind and frost. Only such a man could have worked out the thinking of National Socialism. He knew what it meant when he spoke about the honor of work, and the masses understood him exactly. This is the mysterious bond that exists between the German worker and his Führer. He freed him from his slave existence and gave him back the honor of being a free man. Thus today National Socialism is firmly and securely established in the realm of labor. It is therefore only to be expected that on the national holiday of the German people, May 1, the Führer should receive the delegation of German workers in the Chancellery, and in it the whole German working class, the creative men of mind and fist. From all districts of the Reich they come, in airplanes and by train, to the great hotels of the metropolis. To the Führer they bring the gifts of German labor, greetings from their comrades and the assurance of their fidelity, their love and their faith. They remain at his side until they go out with him to join in the great celebration of German Labor Day.

Still there are many details that have to be improved. Here and there are blunders and difficulties resulting from want and from a lack of understanding. Even disappointments are not lacking, and the workers' material situation has to be improved. Selfishness and vulgarity are still widespread in some places, and the new Gospel of the honor of work is not always received willingly. But all of these are only peripheral. This is not of any concern for the worker, since the word stands and the word must be allowed to stand, *i.e*, the word about the aristocracy of work. Only with

Young workers with the Führer in the Chancellery, May 1, 1934.

On the dockyard of Blohm & Voss, 1934.

Party Day, 1935. The Führer with Dr. Ley, talking to the work-squads.

The Führer at the motor car exhibition in Berlin, 1935.

Cornerstone laying for the new Reich's Bank building, May 5, 1934.

Visit to the Bavarian Motor Works.

The Mercedes-Benz racing car built to the Führer's specifications.

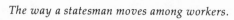

The way a statesman moves among workers.

The work-service of a land-reclamation project.

A visit to a factory. A representative from personnel greets the Führer.

A visit to the Rhineland-Westphalia industrial area.

*International Motor Car Exhibition in Berlin, 1935:
the Protector of the Auto Industry.*

such thinking can one understand the activity of the German Work-Front. Earlier on there was little concern for the condition of places where the German worker created for his people. Today "Schönheit der Arbeit" ("Beauty of Work") takes care that the German creative man may finish his work in worthy places and not in junk rooms. Today through "Kraft dursh Freude" ("Strength through Joy") the German worker has rest and a vacation. Today he goes to the mountains or the sea. Today, and often for the first time, he can wander through his beautiful Fatherland. Today he goes on his own ships to the charm of the lands and seas of the South and into the noble beauty of the North. Today he can enjoy like every German fellow-countryman the imposing achievement of German Dramatic Art and of German music, German orchestras, the best German opera, theater and films. The utility radio set enables him to enjoy that medium, and he can therefore follow every kind of sport today. But pleasure-craving, dissipation and impulsiveness are not the make-up of his new existence. Rather he is oriented towards the lofty and genuine satisfaction found in exercise, in nature and in culture. If a person works hard, he can rejoice all the more since he gives so much more to the people from the results of his work. Nor does the scourge of unemployment still cripple the people. Millions have already found work and they occupy a very special place in the guardianship of the whole nation. The people in charge are concerned that the worker's right to life and his honor not be affected and the foreman is therefore accountable for the welfare of his workers, since they work jointly with him for progress in what they do. Here we have mentioned the basic distinction that differentiates National Socialism from the past: the past knew only chiefs and a multitude of other people. There were chairmen of boards of directors, of administrative boards, of parties, of trade unions, of employers' associations, of social relief funds, and of strike committees. Today we have the Führer, the leader of all the people, and then behind the Führer the leaders of each particular division or group of men. Earlier, one person presided for all the rest. They all presided, they all had no goal and no direction. Today they do have a direction, a path and a goal. Everybody is on the march behind the Führer.

In speech and in words the total difference between the two times is also expressed.

Everyone knows that there is only one man to thank for all this, Adolf Hitler. He created National Socialism, and put the common good ahead of the individual good. The class struggle, whether from above or below, from the right or the left, was raised up by him with the proclamation of the honor of work and of service in the people themselves. That this lesson that made the German Worker the supporter of the State be never lost, the National Socialist Work Service takes care to see that every man who before worked for his own profit now must use his creative hands for the profit of the people.

From Germany the Führer drove out arrogance and contempt, envy and hatred, in work and in property. He made a present to the people of pride and honor in being a worker, as well as the responsibility of serving the totality. The German worker today is happy to be a free man in his own country. He is the first worker of the world. Coming centuries will look back on him with envy. However, from the bottom of his heart he thanks the man who gave him all this, Adolf Hitler.

German peasants greeting their Führer, Adolf Hitler, Bückeberg, 1935.

At the Berlin Philharmonic. The Führer at a concert of the Philharmonic Orchestra under the direction of Generalmusicdirector Wilhelm Furtwängler.

The Führer and The Arts

Dr. Joseph Goebbels

Art is the noblest activity of the human soul and imagination. It is feeling that has become form. What the artist harbors in his heart he brings to expression in art. Heightened feelings postulate heightened modes of expression. He is capable of releasing the voice of his inner *daimon*. What the masses often only have as a dark and gloomy yearning, the artist expresses in Word, Music, Stone or Marble. Art has always exalted and impressed people. He brings them out of the dark humdrum of everyday existence into a better world. Indeed, whole eras of a new cultural and historical evolution have become enlightened and immortalized through it.

Therefore, artists as divinely inspired interpreters of the deepest secrets of human life have always stood in the company of the Great in all other areas as well. It was always the noblest rule

of the true blossom-time of human culture and history for "the singer to walk with the king."

But it should not be said that ascending historical epochs necessarily contain in themselves great artistic potential. On the contrary. More often than not one follows the other. Either a blossoming of the arts and sciences precedes great historical metamorphoses or great historical metamorphoses bring a blossoming of the arts and sciences after them. The reason for this may well be that depending upon the particular time structure, one or the other brings along with it a surpassing and explosive nature arising from either politics or art, and therefore brings out in the other certain static possibilities that were either unknown or not utilized.

However, there is no universally valid law. There have been statesmen who were far removed from the arts. They were so totally absorbed and involved in the technical that they had no time, talent, preference or pleasure to spare for something that was only of intuitive value. They lacked that deep capacity for sympathetic understanding of the real substance of art, which is necessary to serve it with warmth and passion and to become overpowered by it.

There were also many great soldiers who were nothing more than soldiers and wanted to be nothing more. We mean here those great organizers, instructors, educators, and those monumental army corporals whose rise and marching-steps shocked the world. Such statesmen and soldiers brought in the historical evolution which did not directly escape the artistic but was only indirectly concerned with it.

Yet in contrast there are those statesmen and soldiers whose being and behavior are based less on the intellect than on feeling, and their strength comes more from the imagination than from rational knowledge. These are the real greats in the shaping of history. They stand next to art, since they are made of the same elements, and they are the appointed and blessed interpreters of fate for succeeding generations, a fate which governed them and guided them over the centuries.

In our German history, to this category of great historical figures belong men like Frederick I and the great Field Marshall von Moltke. By nature and heredity they had sensitive artistic natures and as the comrades of God they stood at the loom of time. By their irresistibly overpowering command they put their stamp on a development. While not

On the occasion of the arrival of a valuable manuscript acquired by the Führer, he examines the treasures of the Bavarian State Library.

A visit in a Munich artist's studio.
At Professor Wackerle's. In the middle is Frau Professor Troost.

Visit to the Schiller House in Weimar, 1934.

saying anything against the other kind of statesmanly or soldierly activity which is basically derived from technology, this kind of temperament controls to the last refinement with knowledge, diligence, energy and tenacity. Without having had a soldier and civil servant like Frederick William I as a forerunner, a Frederick the Great is unthinkable. One was necessary for the other to live a full life historically. One had to construct the state which the other shaped. One had to have established and trained the army so that the other could put it into motion and lead it in difficult and courageous campaigns to historical victories.

Yet in this connection, we also must not overlook the fact that where both factors are not united in one person the ideal person is more highly valued historically than the purely organizational person, so that the ideal person himself finally produces an artistic offspring which inclines towards the deepest and most secret intuitions. The Frederick who wrote poetry and delved into the most probing philosophical questions, also sat by the bivouac fires in a tattered and soiled uniform among his Grenadiers. He also knew how to hold the flute elegantly just as he understood how to wield the sword with bravery and strength.

The Prusso-German army has never lacked such soldiers. The caricature of Prussian militarism that the world has imputed to us and mechanically repeated had to do with nothing less than the truth. Consequently, those soldiers who passed through the schools of the War Academy or of the General Staff, often were not only military men, but also philosophers by avocation. Nowhere could one find a clearer and more artistic style written than in these army training institutions.

The Führer in Bayreuth.

Certainly German politics has always been poor in such enthusiastic and fascinating personalities. It frequently had good craftsmen who understood their subject, although they more often than not wore themselves out in their business. As a model soldier, Frederick the Great has a vast number of like-minded and similarly oriented people in our history. But in his rôle as a statesman he stands completely alone.

What was great and unique about him was that he placed art beyond the circle of purely esthetic enjoyment. For him it was not a flight from life, but rather a flight before life; of course, when life would become so difficult and unbearable, he had to derive strength and vigor from other quarters so as to remain in control. Art is not weak and does not therefore train people to be weak. Its strong precepts make and keep people strong. Men who are most deeply steeped in it and apply the great lessons of politics and soldierly strategy, behave here as true artists as well and in this sense politics and army leadership are both arts. One art among many others, and they are also always most deeply related to and united with art itself.

As a statesman the Führer belongs among these men in Prusso-German history with such extraordinary and exceptional natures. His deepest self escapes to the artistic. By heredity he is a master-builder, and, as he later laughingly said, he once had the intention in his youth to be a builder, without knowing certainly that one day fate would indeed call him to build not houses but a State. But also his rebuilding of the Reich in its basics allows the eternal laws of true architecture to reappear. His organization of the State is brought about by a quite obviously effective logic.

The Führer leaves an artist's studio in the Academy of Painting Arts in Munich.

Visitors to the Bayreuth festival greet the Führer.

Sketches of Front-Soldier Hitler: Ardoye in Flanders (summer, 1917).

It is accomplished after extensive and well thought through planning, without precipitation and nervousness. A good master-builder, who knows that Rome was not built in a day, also knows that he is called to work and to create not for a limited time but for decades or centuries. This directly sets apart the new formation of the Reich by the Führer from all previous attempts. It is based on durability. In it there is a curious and almost architectural clarity. And by its appropriateness and beauty it is united in a rare harmony.

Once, long before he came to power, the Führer said in a speech: "If the German artist knew what I would later do for them, they would stand by me!" These words are now bruited about in the wind; without remembering some impatient creditors, the Führer made good earlier than had been hoped.

How strongly related to inner necessity art is for him! One could already surmise this from before the time he took power. With the most difficult political negotiations or the most grinding tactical battles facing him, in the evening alone or with a few comrades-in-arms he could often be seen in a quiet loge of a theater listening to the augmented tempo of a Wagnerian music drama and perceiving its artistic consonance with his political being. Today, only a few people heard as often as he (to single out an example) "Die Meistersinger" or "Tristan." He is a fanatic for artistic investigation. He does no homage to that bourgeois self-complacency that thinks it understands and grasps a genius once it has seen or heard something. He is filled with that deep and almost submissive respect for the blessed greatness of the original in art that has taken possession of a man.

This respect sees and understands a man and his work as a unit. One has to have seen the Führer in a circle of artists in order to understand how deeply and personally related he feels himself to be to them. One has had to have the opportunity to observe his indefatigable solicitude for art and artists in their daily activity in order to understand what this means both for himself and his history-making work. To a certain degree his respect for true value and work is a kind of metamorphosed gratitude. For example, what his position as patron and directly concerned friend means for the work of Richard Wagner in general and for Bayreuth in particular is known only by those who have the joy to be able to help him.

For the little circle that tends to be around him there are unforgettable hours that cling to the memory in which the Führer, still only the leader of the opposition, jotted down with a runaway pencil on loose pages the grandiose plans for the architectural rebuilding of Berlin and Munich. Here everything was in its exact place. Modern technological thinking was connected with the latest in architectural competence. This was the archetype of what these cities would look like when cleansed and purified of the false characteristics imprinted on them by a styleless and tasteless age.

The monumental Party buildings, the rebuilding of the Königsplatz and the German Art Museum in Munich as well as the already projected grandiose transformation of the capital of the Reich, are the first visible accomplishments of this new charming and fanciful advance planning. To the outsider it seems almost inconceivable that the Führer gives not only the stimulus and initiative to these for-centuries-planned projects, but that he also controlled and pursued professionally the tiniest details. The Führer always has time for a building plan. How often could we have observed him in the studio of the prematurely deceased architect Professor Troost, enthusing over plans and models which have now become stone-upon-stone realities. How often we were able to accompany him to new buildings at their various stages of development and to verify his deep joy over the smallest detail which might seem senseless and purposeless in the overall.

Also the pictures he painted in his youth breathe this same spirit. They are most carefully drawn to the last stroke and betray the precision and the accuracy of a specialist master-builder. It may be said that there are able counterfeiters who can effect a falsification and a copying of such small artworks with an unequalled virtuosity, but they could never deceive the real connoisseur. One of the Führer's real pictures is easy to distinguish from a false one on first sight. From the genuine one the Führer speaks, and if only in seed, there are present all the artistic precepts which the Führer showed in his building of a State with his historical and monumental consequences.

The same man, who in his young days in Vienna gave up an untold number of lunches and dinners in order to get standing room at the Vienna Opera House to hear Wagner or Mozart, has the same artistic passion today for a painting or a piece of sculpture. A stroke of luck enables him to acquire Böcklin's "Battle of the Centaurs," and we now see him sitting quietly and for a long time

Sketches of Front-Soldier Hitler: Dug-out in Fournes.

Watercolor of Front-Soldier Hitler: Ruins of a monastery in Messines (December, 1914).

Watercolor of Front-Soldier Hitler: House with white fence.

A watercolor of the Führer's from 1914: The courtyard of the old Residence in Munich.

with compassion and humility, looking at the greatness of true artistry in this painterly projection of a genius.

Who would question that these noble passions are only almost obligatorily working forms of expression of his artistic perception which also appear in the emergence of his historical work? Are not his speeches evidence of his artistic intuition? Do they not work in their construction, in the clarity of their style, in the monumentality of their thought progression, in the precision and multiplicity of their expression, in the same way as a classical monument or a Bach fugue? To understand him in a simple human way is impossible. Here is united the particular-to-the-general picture which gives us in a totality the contours of a man who perceives and behaves in an artistically intuitive manner, a man who is and works in everything just as he must be and must work, and he is incapable of acting otherwise.

From its beginning the Führer has inspired his Movement to that hot impulse of modern activity which later gave strength to its great victory. He has not given in to technology, but rather consciously put technology in his service. The Führer then is a supporter of technology. He uses its achievements to solve his problems. And technol-

ogy has its artistic side. A nobly built bridge, or an automobile built in accordance with almost classic laws of esthetics always satisfies a person's sense of the beautiful. The highways which the Führer sketched and which modern engineers built after his plans, are 20th-century art works. Again, on a sunny Sunday afternoon in front of the great monumental curve of the Mangfall Bridge we can see the Führer standing and reflecting with pride and contentment and reflecting on the most modern technical achievements and their eternal artistic origin.

The Führer is the sworn enemy of dilettantism; he embraces the proud prospect that things be remunerative. He would see, hear or read about greatness 10 times rather than come in contact with an article of mediocre quality or less even once. If he is shown a film that exhibits an artistic bent, he wants it shown to him a second time. Mediocre films will be cut off after five or 10 minutes.

Is it any wonder that all real artists love him and honor him from their hearts? He is their friend after all, and when necessary their generous protector. He himself could not conceive of a life without art. No royal Maecenas was ever as generous to the arts as he. When they are great and promising for the future, he lends them his encouraging hand. Nothing is more foreign to him than being patronizing. He had a very difficult path to art as a destitute construction worker. With the greatest material sacrifices he finally reached his goal after hard fighting. He therefore opens his heart and his hand to everyone and brings art to the people and the people to art. Ideas such as having a "People's Theater" became a reality under his leadership. The great German cultural organization "Kraft durch Freude" finds in him a most warm-hearted friend. He is a counsellor and trusted superviser. His sense of beauty does not have that disagreeable esthetic trait of hedonistic egotism. He gives meaning both to the purposeless and the universal alike.

Before too long statesmen from other countries visited him in Berlin and became involved for days in difficult negotiations with him on the question of European reconstruction. They had no idea that the same man who was defending the German right to live, and who was therefore almost a political economist or a military specialist who seemed to shake each document or piece of information from his sleeve, would, on the same evening, be sitting deeply moved listening to the quintet from the third act of "Meistersinger" or to a song of Schubert, Schumann or Wolf. Perhaps they have believed that now suddenly this man had become someone completely different, who wears a new face unknown to them; and yet he remained the same in actuality, a statesman whose scope is almost immeasurable, a man who contains in himself all the characteristics and capabilities of the German soul, an artist who sat among artists and who felt one with them, since he carried a part of them in himself. Perhaps this hour gave everyone who could participate a deeper insight into the Führer's inmost spirit than

one could get from technical discussions and conferences. Here again appeared that fascinating force of a real personality, such as that of the great Prussian king, which enabled him to fight through and to stand his ground in his different wars while also writing poetry, being a friend to philosophy, building Sans Souci, playing the flute and if the work of being a statesman and a soldier left any time, entertaining the most illustrious and the finest minds of Europe around his table. Out of these apparent contradictions and contrasts was formed the ultimate synthesis of a great human reality and operation that will survive the centuries. Here we have the artistic translated into the soldierly. There is the same living force working in different spheres. It uses the same kinetic energies that also propel and accelerate art: imagination, instinct, inspiration, grace and administrative ability. Perhaps a later age, in viewing the whole situation, might be able to consider what this means for Germany and their fate as a nation. Good luck is with us. There is a true genius amongst us, with us and around us to experience and to perceive. Here the artistic sensibilities of a great man are no longer the need of luxury or of passing the time. Here it is a need truly speaking for being, living and working.

Perhaps the best and deepest way to understand the Führer is if one sees him in the midst of these realities. At this point art for him is that secret power which in all the gray hours in which we are ensnared kindles a new love in the human heart.

And his association with art and artists, his solicitude and tireless care and control are nothing else for them than the expiation and redemption of a debt and an obligation which the poet refers to when he says: "Thou gracious art, I thank thee for him."

The speaker's rostrum on the grounds of the Reich's Party Assembly in Nuremberg.

The Führer's Buildings

Architect Albert Speer

History has often seen heads of state giving support to the arts and to architecture in particular. A rococo prince of the 18th century invested money to make the sight of his castles and gardens a welcome one and in his time he made it possible for living architects to create freely.

The Führer too builds as a head of state but he could never build in this delegated fashion. Consequently, his great constructions which are beginning to rise in many places today are an essential expression of the thousand-year Movement and are, therefore, a part of the Movement itself. At any rate, the Führer built this Movement.

Through its strength he came to power and still today he determines its direction down to the smallest detail. From now on he can no longer build like a head of state from bygone centuries nor even less like a Maecenas. He must build like a National Socialist. As such he commands, just as he commands the purpose and the expression of the Movement, the neatness and the purity of the manner of building, the severity of expression, the nobility of materials and, most importantly, the new inner meaning and the inner character of his buildings.

For the Führer architecture is no mere pastime.

The "Eternal Watch" in the Königsplatz in Munich.

It is, rather, a most earnest concern of the National Socialist Movement to make its great expression also in stone.

Something unique was to happen in the history of the German people. At a certain decisive turning point the Führer started out not only with the greatest ideological New Order of our history, but also with singular expertise as a master-builder. He created stone buildings which are sure to give evidence not only of a political inclination but also of a cultural capability for making something that will cause our people's age of greatness to last a thousand years.

After many centuries of confusion a clarity and a strength will give an architectural direction that, as it further develops, will produce a completely new architectural feeling in what is to follow.

In addition to social questions, the Führer from his youth has been also deeply concerned with architecture, as can be seen from what he wrote in MEIN KAMPF in 1924:

"Once my interest in social questions was awakened, I began to study them with greater thoroughness. It was a new and until then unknown world that revealed itself to me. It was natural that I should have so ardently responded to my love for architecture. To me, with the excep-

tion of music, it was the queen of the arts. In this light my pursuit of it was not 'work', but rather the greatest happiness. Until late into the night I was able to read or draw without getting tired. This greatly enforced my belief that my beautiful dream of the future, however many years distant, would indeed become a reality. I was quite convinced that someday I would make a name for myself as a master-builder."

The importance of these influences on him during his years in Vienna is mentioned by him in the first chapter of MEIN KAMPF:

"At that time I fashioned for myself a theory of life and an ideology that became the granite-like basis of my behavior. Once I had made something, I did not have to change anything basic, but only do a little research.

"On the contrary.

"I firmly believe today that what I felt basically in my youth is still present with me."

The Führer never gave up this youthful enthusiasm for architecture. But war and revolution deeply shook German political and national life. As a soldier Hitler had become more involved in political questions and finally decided to become a politician.

He said, "Is it not ridiculous to want to build houses on such a foundation?"

For him becoming a politician was a holy duty. It was a difficult but necessary decision to bid farewell to architecture, the art to which he inwardly always remained faithful, an art which continues to involve him and which is his great love today.

During the first troubled years of his political struggle, along with the organization of the Movement, he also gave a definitive and artistically clear form to its symbolic means of expression. He sketched out the swastika flag of the Movement and therefore also the national flag of the German people. He decided to use as the party's symbol the national eagle, which therefore became the national emblem of the German Reich. He also gave form to the standards of the Storm Troopers and the SS. He evolved a modern organization out of the many demonstrations and determined the basic idea for all the buildings for the Reich's Party Celebration in Nuremberg.

He outlined and determined through many painstaking conferences at the Party congress in Nuremberg, not only its basic rules and program, but in lengthy reflections he also gave the exact layouts for the installation of each of the groupings of the Party and for the line-up of the banners and the setup of each of the assembly rooms. Some of the Führer's sketches and drawings from this period are preserved in Nuremberg. For him art is his highest objective. It is never "work", but always his "greatest happiness".

It was at just the right time that he met his ar-

The Königsplatz in Munich after its rebuilding by Adolf Hitler.

The portico of the House of German Art in Munich.

Model for the Congress Hall on the grounds of the Reich's Party Assembly in Nuremberg.

The Führer and Rudolf Hess visiting the construction site of the Munich Führerhaus.

chitect. It was Paul Ludwig Troost with whom he soon developed a natural and binding friendship. What Dietrich Eckart was for the Führer in the exchange of thoughts on ideology, Professor Troost soon became in architecture.

Through the unprecedented bond of these two men a first building sprang up. It was the "little building" of the Movement, the "Brown House" in the Briennerstrasse in Munich. Although this was only a reconstruction, as the Führer later often mentioned, it was a stupendous undertaking for that time.

Now we can see everything. What might have seemed to be harsh when he came to power can now be understood. It is never monotonous. There is simplicity and clarity without false embellishment. Taste is economically expressed. Superfluousness is unthinkable. Materials are the finest in form and line.

The plans for this construction evolved in the same simple atelier of Professor Troost, in the back room of a house in Munich's Theresienstrasse. Later, in the same place, the foundation of a new architectural feeling was laid, in the plans for the Königsplatz in Munich as well as the Art Museum and many other buildings inspired by the Führer. The Führer never let these plans remain in his office files.

For years (and now still in his free time) he made trips to Troost's studio. Here, far from his work in politics, he was able to become intellectually absorbed in the plans for new buildings. It was not only with the broad over-all plans that the Führer busied himself. He was concerned with every detail and with every new use of material, his encouragement and appraisal were felt. As the Führer has often acknowledged, these hours of joint planning have been hours of the purest joy

and the deepest happiness, the most noble relaxation, in which he continued to find new strength. Here, in the few free hours politics leaves him, he can dedicate himself to architecture.

For the many years before he assumed power, Hitler had been speaking about plans for buildings which only today have become realities. As early as the winter of 1931–32, he had discussed plans for the future building of the Königsplatz in Munich and we have many of these sketches that remain from this period.

When the Glass Palace burned down in Munich in 1932, the Government made an insignificant attempt at its rebuilding. But even before coming to power the Führer was deeply concerned about this uncompleted plan. When one compares a model of this earlier plan to his final sketch of the now-completed House of German Art, one can clearly see the ideal world that is formed by the Führer's buildings. And this new world received its impetus from a sketch by Paul Ludwig Troost.

In Paul Ludwig Troost the Führer had found his master architect. Troost knew how to understand his intentions and to express them always in the correct architectural style.

In his great discourse at the culture convention at the 1935 Party Convention the Führer erected a grander monument to Professor Troost than one could ever imagine for a contemporary architect. He said, "It should fill us with joyful pride that a master architect, the greatest Germany has seen since Schinkel, would by special providence have erected this first and, unfortunately, the only monumental work for the Reich and for the Party in such a noble and truly Germanic architectural style."

It gives the Führer great joy to see his planning of a building realized. And it is an equally great

The Führer leaving the construction site of the House of German Art.

joy for him to be able to experience the building's growth.

As he wanders, often only in the company of a few fellow workers, through his building sites, he is a complete and total expert. His frequent questions about the foundation, the strength of walls and various construction details usually uncover some already existing problem. Frequently, after the people involved have long been deliberating the possibility of a solution to a question on a particular construction site, he comes up with a suggestion, mostly without precedent, which always shows itself to be clear and practicable.

Every new building, each new detail, has the Führer's closest attention with his thorough examination and assessment. Yet, with his joy in minute details, he still never forgets the over-all idea and the special unity that distinguishes all of his buildings.

The Führer's buildings were all built out of natural stone after craftsmen-tested principles. Natural stone and Nordic bricks are our most durable construction materials. Here he feels that, despite the initial expense, such materials prove to be cheaper in the long run. Durability is always the most decisive element. After thousands of years the Führer's buildings will still be speaking about our time. The imperishable buildings of the Movement and of the State will be standing in the cities of Germany as long as buildings stand and they will be a source of pride to each individual, knowing that they belong to him. It is not the apartment buildings or the administration buildings or the banks that will give character to the cities, but rather the buildings the Führer himself created and designed.

With regard to the way cities have been in the past and will be in the future, the Führer writes:

"In the 19th century our cities began more and more to lose their character as cultural centers and to be nothing more than mere human settlements. Even when Munich was a city of only 60,000, it was already on the way to becoming one of the first centers of art in Germany. Today almost all factory towns have reached this population, if they have not already surpassed that number, and they can be proud that they manifest the genuine value of true cities without stinting on the private and public housing. But without distinction. It is puzzling how such a lack of distinction should be so much a part of such towns as these. No one will be particularly proud of a town which has nothing really to offer, lacks individuality and has no concern for art.

"But this is not enough. Large towns are growing in population and they are proportionately increasingly poorer in works of art.

"What our great cities have given over to culture is completely inadequate. All of our cities exist on the glory and greatness of the past.

"Today our metropolises have no treasures at all, even though there is the possibility of having great monuments and landmarks everywhere. In the past almost every town had a special monument of which it could be proud. The uniqueness of the ancient city lay not in private buildings but in the public monuments which were built not for the moment but for all time. They did not reflect the wealth of an individual but rather expressed the greatness and importance of the general public.

"In the German Middle Ages the same guiding principle existed, although under quite different circumstances. The Acropolis or the Pantheon of antiquity have now become the Gothic cathedral.

"How truly wretched today is the proportion

The lobby of the German Opera House in Charlottenburg. The Führer cooperated on its reconstruction.

The Führer, Professor Gall and Architect Speer visiting the building site of the House of German Art in Munich.

between public and private construction! If Berlin were to suffer the same fate as Rome, her descendants might consider that her great works were the stores of the Jews or the great business houses, and that they were the expression of the characteristic culture of our day.

"Our cities today are greatly lacking in outstanding monuments to the people and the community and it is no wonder that people find no representations of themselves in their own towns."

It is in this sense, then, that we must understand the great buildings of the Führer in the Königsplatz, the House of German Art in Munich and the Party buildings in Nuremberg. They are a beginning, and no small one indeed. We are now standing with the Führer's buildings at the beginning of a new evolution.

The sense that the Führer gives to construction today makes us always think of greater and more impressive buildings.

However, we must not be deceived into thinking that with these buildings the Führer's work is completed.

On the contrary.

From his own speeches we know what great value Hitler places on the social circumstances of all Germans and on the fact that each individual can take personal pride in what the community as a whole has done. The great importance the Führer gave to housing conditions can be seen from MEIN KAMPF. In his years in Vienna he had got to know the living conditions of the workers. He wrote:

"What I had not anticipated at that time, I quickly learned and understood: The question of the nationalization of a people is above all a question of the creation of healthy social conditions as the basis for the education and formation of the individual."

The official statistics for the completed housing either with new buildings or with reconversion for the territory of the Reich are:

1932	159,121
1933	202,113
1934	319,439

These figures say more than any words how the building of safe housing has increased under the Führer's leadership. And this increase will continue and become even greater when the massive building projects have been completed, something which is essential for us and which "cannot be put off".

At this point, when the housing projects for the workers have been completed and clean factories erected, our great metropolises will build the monuments of National Socialism the way the cathedrals of the Middle Ages were built above the gables of the private houses.

The basic tasks that have to be completed are immense, but the Führer gave us all the proper spirit and courage when he told us in his talk at the cultural session of the Reich's Party Assembly:

"With such exalted tasks men will grow. We have no right to doubt that if the Almighty gives us the courage to require the impossible, he will give our people the strength and ability to do the impossible and to accomplish something that will not die."

A visit to the new mountain road in the Alps.

Adolf Hitler and His Roads

General Inspector Dr. Fritz Todt

Whoever has come to know the Führer in the previous essays as a statesman, an orator, the leader of the Movement and in his daily life, might, when he reads the title of this essay, ask the question: Does this statesman, this politician, this head of the German Reich in this very disturbed age really have such a personal interest and the available time to become personally involved with such an abstract technical subject as road building? The following notes will give an indication as to just how involved the Führer is with his roads.

The Idea

As far back as his imprisonment at Landsberg the Führer had spoken about the need to have roads built which would be technically suited for automobile travel and which would also bring together all the individual areas of Germany. In his 14 years of political struggle the Führer used the motor car exclusively in his travels and he got to know the German roads from north to south and from east to west. We are all the more astounded at the Führer's knowledge of road plans, the character and condition of the roads as well as their resting places and peculiarities. The Führer especially values automobile travel since no other mode of transportation is able to link up the traveler with the people as closely. Someone once attempted to figure out how many kilometers the Führer had traveled over the 14 years of his political struggle. It was at least 500,000 to 700,000 and probably more. The Führer's journeys on the German country roads add up to 12 or 15 times the circumference of the earth. Even before coming to power, on these trips he developed his mature idea of the necessity of creating a network of roads that would be open to motor traffic.

Twelve days after he was named Reich's Chancellor, at the opening of the automobile show on February 11, 1933, the Führer made his first public speech, and besides some other aspects of the promotion of motorization, he announced the inauguration of a far-reaching plan for road construction:

"Just as bridle paths were built and railroads laid out in accordance with need, so automobile traffic now demands special roadways. Just as we used to measure distances between people in the past by the railroad, in the future we shall be measuring by highways."

Scarcely three months went by since that February 11th, filled with the joy of the celebration of

Summer, 1935. The Mangfall Bridge.

taking power on January 30th, until we had the first National Labor Day in the young National Socialist Reich. On this spring day the sun climbed even higher in the sky for the German people. The Führer spoke about this as he did about the departure from the previous confusion; of the elimination of unemployment; of the honor and glory of work; of the beginning of collective labor, which was based on the will; the requirements and the groundwork for the strengthening of a nation. Towards the end of this first speech about the beginning construction of the Reich, the Führer spoke these words:

"We are proposing a program that we do not want to have to leave to our posterity, the program of building and rebuilding our roads, a gigantic task that will demand billions. We shall clear away the opposition and make a great beginning."

Therefore this May 1st was also the Inauguration Day for the road-building program. Out of the Führer's idea came the will to accomplish.

In the subsequent weeks the Führer received specialists in construction both from Germany and abroad to inform him and he demanded a law from the cabinet to realize his plans. Resistance to his words of May 1st was finally overcome by many and frequent discourses. On June 28th the Cabinet concluded the law on setting up the "Reichsautobahnen" Enterprise. A few days afterward in a period of scarcely three minutes the Inspector General of the German Roadways was named.

Road marking at the beginning of the Munich-to-the-frontier highway.

The Inspector General's Initiation

In 1933 the hottest summer day in Berlin was certainly July 5th. For weeks on end the summer heat had been keeping the stones of the capital so

The opening of the first stretch of the Munich-frontier highway.

The Führer's interest in road construction.
A visit to the mountain road.

warm that even the short nights brought no relief. As on every other day, interviews with the Reich's Chancellor began about 10 a.m. in the Reich's Chancellery. He held these meetings, with a brief respite at noon, until late into the night. Ministers, gauleiters, delegations of workers, industrialists, Germans living abroad and many others spent their time, hour after hour, in presenting the Führer with their ideas. In the antechamber many promised not to speak more than 10 minutes, but the Führer himself would take hold of their theme, take a position, elucidate the questions from the ground up and was as interested in the last presentation late at night just as keenly as in the first.

The newly-named Inspector General was summoned for his briefing by the Führer at 1 p.m. As so often happens, the morning schedule was prolonged by lengthy discourses. Finally the waiting period ended at 5 p.m. with the announcement, "The Chancellor will speak with you since he at last has the time."

When, after the next-to-the-last visitor, the Inspector General was announced shortly before 9 p.m., the Chancellor said, "Come and take a walk with me in the garden. I have to get some fresh air." During the hour-and-a-half walk in the Reich's Chancellery garden the Führer briefed the Inspector General on his ideas. He spoke about the coming developments in the traffic systems, about their present inadequacy, about the need for taking immediate measures, about building and constructing on a broad scale. He warned about obstacles and difficulties. He set up the technical details and made precise decisions as to the road widths whose design was of the highest priority. He determined in general terms the lines

One of the Führer's highways.

His roads bring Adolf Hitler to the people.

of the central road network and finally left the Inspector General by repeating, "I believe in the necessity of this action and in the correctness of this beginning, and you must believe in it just as strongly as I and staunchly act accordingly."

The First Ground-Breaking, Frankfurt-am-Main, September 23, 1933

In two-and-a-half months of most intensive work plans were made. For the beginning of this work, which was to extend over the whole of Germany, Frankfurt-am-Main was suggested. Years before a group had been there studying a theoretical plan for a straight highway from Hamburg through Frankfurt to Basel. Their preplanning made it easy for an accelerated completion of the designs. By the beginning of September the plans for the first stretch from Frankfurt to Darmstadt were ready. The ground-breaking and therefore the beginning of the whole enormous project were set for September 23rd. In his first conversations with the Inspector General the Führer had decided that he himself would inaugurate the project.

For years the number of those out of work in Frankfurt had been increasing until it reached some 80,000 in 1932. Now the Führer's master construction-operation was going on right next to this city. This gave thousands of workers permanent work and thereby brought something to trust and believe in to the life of the worker and his dependents. About 7 a.m. the first 700 workers marched off from the labor office. At the Börsenplatz (Stock Market Square) the Gauleiter and the Inspector General were distributing their tools. Music and jubilation from the line of workers extended to the Main River, their new place of work.

The Führer arrived at 10 a.m. by plane. The Führer's trip through the streets of Frankfurt was fraught with the greatest difficulties: The barricaded Storm Troopers were shouting and hailing the Führer and the citizens of Frankfurt, old and young, were coming through the barricades in ever-increasing numbers, so that the trip from the airport to the work site took more than an hour.

The place of the first ground-breaking was no festival square but rather just a construction site. The workers and their relatives were standing in front of the embankment from which the Führer spoke: The guests of honor here were given somewhat short shrift since the real guests of honor were the workers themselves. The Führer spoke these words:

"Today we stand at the beginning of a mighty task. Its significance will not only be for the German traffic system, but in the broadest sense in later decades, its greatest worth will be seen in the German economy itself . . .

"In decades to come people will see that communication will be dependent upon these new great highways that we will build throughout the whole of Germany . . .

"I know that this festive day makes us forget that the time will come when rain, frost and snow will make work for the individual worker sour and difficult. But it is imperative that the work be done. No one helps us if we do not help ourselves."

The Führer ended his speech, saying, "Now go to your work! Construction must begin today! And ere years have past, a mammoth work must give witness of our will, our diligence, our talent and our strength of purpose. German workers, to work!"

Amidst the jubilation of the workers after these words the Führer took up his shovel and went to the construction track. An automobile transportation truck roared up, filled high with 2-cubic-meter-wagons. The wagons made loud noises as they were unloaded onto the platform, which was to be installed at the foot of the 6-meter-high embankment. The Führer's spade went heftily into the hard lump of earth. Thrust after thrust. This was no symbolic shovelful but real excavation work! A few workers recognized that the Führer had not stopped until a 2-cubic-meter space had been dug. They jumped up with their shovels to help him. The Führer shoveled along with them until the piles of earth had reached their proper height and until the first drops of sweat fell from his forehead to the ground. Laughingly, with his two unknown fellow workers, the Führer stopped since there was nothing more to shovel. As he went through the other work sites he found that the more than 700 workers had begun their work with him.

"Did you see how the Führer at the end shoveled the earth away from the track so that the wagons could be refilled? Just like a real construction worker! He can work. I'm scarcely able to keep up with him," said one of the two workers later.

In the week after that ground-breaking an observer came to the Bauleiter (Director) of the Reich's Highways and said, "Counsellor (Herr Oberbaurat), we have to fence in the place where the Führer did his shoveling. On their day off our workers are taking pocketsful of earth home with them. Even the women and children are doing it."

Thus the work of the Führer's and the workers' way of thinking ennobles a kind of work which till now had been called filthy. Many workers' families from Frankfurt still cherish today a packet of this earth as a valued possession.

Collaborating with the Führer

Normally the Führer kept in very close touch with the Inspector General about the progress of his work. Therefore, the Führer with his competence involved himself in many details in order to influence his collaborator's basic attitude towards this work and to insure that it was done in accordance with his will. It is all the more evident today that in these discussions over details the Führer's decision in the course of time turned out to be the right one.

An example of this was a decision about the lineation of the routes on the southern shore of the Chiemsee in Upper Bavaria. Between this lake and the rising mountains there is a moor several kilometers wide. The difficulties of crossing it had been realized at the time of the building of the railroad. The first sketch of the direction of the Reich's Highway yielded to the moor with a wide curve off from the lake shore to the south. The Führer knew that this route had no view either of the lake or of the mountains, so he was very concerned that a way nearer the lake could be found. In accordance with his suggestions extensive drillings were made in the neighborhood of the lake. Through these investigations we found to our surprise that a special formation right on the lake itself was for a road that followed the wishes of the Führer.

The Führer also repeatedly made the final choice as to the shape of the large bridgeheads. One of the first real big bridges on which construction was started was the Mangfallbrücke near Munich, with a length of 300 meters and a height of 60 meters above the valley. Out of a contest in which 70 designs were entered, the Führer picked the design that was used for construction and established with it the shape for a big bridge. The same was used in several other projects later on. Clear and simple, but at the same time magnificent and daring, are the lines and forms of the structures which the Führer defined. Next to the design, the question of how solid the structure would be strongly influenced his decision. Cheap material like hollow supports and pillars the Führer rejected because he doubted their unlimited durability. His structures, as well as his whole thinking, were not focused on the present but on serving future development. What we build has to be still standing when we are long gone. The decisions of the Führer can also be negative on occasion. His refusal is spoken clearly and the reasons for it stated. On one occasion, the Führer stopped work on a displeasing construction site by calling the inspector on the telephone and ordering an immediate shutdown of the site. The Führer also picked the design for the German Alp road and repeatedly made decisions concerning even the smallest details.

They are seeing the Führer for the first time.

Opening of the Frankfurt-Darmstadt highway, 1935. From left to right: War Minister von Blomberg, the Führer, Inspector General Dr. Todt, Reich's Bank President Dr. Schacht, Director General of the Reich's Highways Dr. Dorpmülk, Reich's Minister Dr. Goebbels.

The Führer on the Rhine at the Saar exhibition in 1934.

The start of construction work in all parts of the German Reich during the year 1934 made it necessary for some of the workers to live in barracks. To begin with, the construction industry put up these work camps in the same fashion that had been established in past centuries. During the summer these barracks were just barely adequate. But at the arrival of winter it looked as if urgent improvement were needed since the sleeping quarters for the workers on Adolf Hitler's roads were totally insufficient. Repeated warnings to the industry about the poor conditions in the camps were partly successful. It was difficult to improve the conditions in the camps quickly and efficiently since everybody was used to deficiencies for years. Eventually the Inspector General informed the Führer about the problems so as to receive further instructions. As soon as the Führer heard that the barracks for his road workers had left a lot to be desired, he made drastic changes within a few hours with the uncompromising energy one expected from him.

With the cooperation of the work force, he erected model camps all over Germany within a few weeks. The worker on Adolf Hitler's roads was moved into the new clean lodgings. He eats in bigger rooms. Each camp has large wash and shower rooms with warm and cold water and a recreation room for entertainment after the day's work is done. The Führer himself designed every detail in the camps. Through the intervention of the Führer in autumn, 1934, the camps of the German workers achieved a standard that no other country in Europe could approach.

To inspect a construction site or a finished stretch of road is one of the biggest joys for the Führer. On the construction site the Führer is interested in everything—the management, the structures, the workers' lodgings and, most of all, the way the road fits into the environment. The Führer likes his roads to be bold and magnificent but, at the same time, they must harmonize with the scenery. The workers were often very surprised about his unexpected visits. Occasionally one or the other dropped his pickax in surprise. But then their eyes shone with happiness over the Führer's visit to their work site. You cannot imagine what feelings of happiness and joy you find on a construction site when you see in the faces of hundreds of grownups total happiness, the likes we are only used to seeing in the faces of children under the Christmas tree. As a rule the workers stay in their assigned locations and continue their work after the first surprise, then they show how really well they can work. The Führer talks to some of them, especially the older workers. Sixty- and 70-year-olds are no rarity in the construction busi-

ness. To a 70-year-old worker near Darmstadt the Führer said, "I wish I could still work as well as you can now, when I am your age."

The Führer is inspired by his first drive over a newly completed stretch of road. The traffic census is of consuming interest to him because it confirms the interest of private and industrial traffic on the new roads. The Führer gave a picnic to honor the opening of the highway between Heidelberg and Frankfurt-am-Main.

He interrupted his travel from Mittelbaden to the Rhineland to make the first drive on this stretch, a few days before it was given over to the general public. After the announcement of the Inspector General, the Führer decided to stop for a rest at a suitable picnic place. In the splendid, autumnal beech forest, the Führer's car fleet left the road. The supply officer Kannenberg arranged a magical table top feast in the forest. After one of these trips over a newly completed roadway section, you can hear from third parties how truly enthusiastically the Führer spoke of the experience.

Adolf Hitler's roads are closely linked with their creator. The Führer himself emphasized over and over the great importance of the finished roadways for the future development of transportation and more. Within a few years, these roads became one of Germany's biggest propaganda issues. Not only because of the very rapidly growing need for transportation and expanding production but also because it attracted hundreds of thousands of foreigners every year to look at the completed highways all over the German Reich. The German highway system became the most modern in the world.

From far beyond the German borders, foreign countries are watching our Führer's road building. Almost every week single people or groups of foreign people are asking for permission to visit the construction sites or the completed stretches of Germany's highway system. They express their enthusiasm and admiration in letters and newspaper articles as they watch the growing of the Führer's masterpiece. One of the many foreign press agencies writes:

"Just as the pyramids tell the stories of the pharaohs, and the Roman streets remind us of the power the Roman Emperor once had, so the beautiful highway system of the German people will remind them forever of the most unusual personality in their history. A fellow German, once without name and position, who created through his own power a new empire and molded through his will the destiny of a nation. All this without any outside help."

In Nuremberg, at the window of the Hotel "Deutscher Hof."

Our Hitler

Radio speech to the German people in honor of the Führer's birthday
BY DR. JOSEPH GOEBBELS

As often as the Führer has to show himself and make speeches at mass rallies, receptions and as spokesman for the party on official occasions, to thousands and hundreds of thousands of people, he avoids all declarations and tributes which are only given in honor of his person. For this reason, he spends all his birthdays in small, unknown German towns and cities. What a strong impression the Führer made on his close colleagues, with his warm human character and personal way, can best be felt in the speeches made by Reich's Minister Dr. Goebbels over all German radio stations to the German people in honor of his birthday. The contents of the third speech on April 20, 1935 especially deserve to be recorded within the pages of this book.

"My fellow German citizens. Two years ago, on April 20, 1933, only three months after Hitler came into power, I made a speech to the German people over the radio in honor of the Führer's birthday. Today, just as in the past, it is not my desire to read a flaming editorial to you. I leave that to people who have more style than I. It is also not my intention to praise the historical work of Adolf Hitler. To the contrary, today, on the birthday of the Führer, I believe it is time to have a look at the human side of Hitler. I want to open the people's eyes to see the whole charm of his personality, his secret magic and the deep, striking power of his individual work. I don't think there is anybody left in the world who does not know him as a politician and a superior popular leader. Only few have the pleasure to be near him daily and observe his human side, to experience him and, I wish to add, because of it, to learn to deeply understand and love him. These few understand the wonder of how and why it was possible for a man who had half the population against him only a short three years ago to be today above all suspicion and criticism from his people. Because, if Germany has found a never-to-be-destroyed unity in one thing, it is the conviction that Adolf Hitler is the man of fate who has the calling within himself to lead the nation up to the much-yearned-for freedom out of the internal disruption and the external political humiliation. That a man in this po-

Memorial service for General Field Marshal von Hindenburg in the courtyard of the Tannenberg monument. The Führer's farewell speech.

Hitler's last visit to Hindenburg before his death in July, 1934.

sition, where it is occasionally necessary to make very hard, unpopular decisions, captured the hearts of his total population is perhaps the deepest, most wonderful secret of our time. This cannot be explained by facts alone because it is most often the people who had to make, and are still making, the biggest sacrifices for him and his national buildup and feel the most deeply and happily about his consignment. They stand behind him, the Führer and the Man, with true and impassioned love. That is the result of his enchanting personal work and the deep magic of his true, unadulterated humaneness. My speech will be about this human side of his, which is clearly seen by the people who are closest to him. Like all real humanity, it is clearly defined in his being and his actions. It is displayed in the smallest, as well as the biggest, things. The simple clarity, which takes form in his political pictures, is also the domineering principle in his whole life. It is unimaginable to picture him striking a pose. There his people would not recognize him. His daily menu is the most plain and modest one you can imagine. It is never changed whether he eats with a few friends or entertains important political visitors. At a reception a short time ago, the district administrator of the Winter Help Factory, a Party member of long standing, asked the Führer after

The morning of January 15, 1935:
the Führer thanking Gauleiter Bürckel for the Saar victory.

lunch please to sign one of the menus for him to keep as a memento. The Führer was perplexed for a moment, then he said laughing, 'It doesn't make any difference. Our menus never expand, so everybody is welcome to look at them.'

Adolf Hitler is one of the few heads of state who never decorates himself with badges of honor and medals. He has only one war decoration which was awarded to him for his outstanding personal courage as a plain soldier. That is the proof of his purposefulness but also of his pride. There is no human under the sun who could honor him except himself. All obtrusiveness is disgusting to him. Where he has to represent the State and his peo-

ple, he does it with awe-inspiring and cool dignity. Behind everything he is and does stand the words the great soldier Schliffen wrote about his work: "To be rather than to seem." This, in alliance with hard work and enduring toughness, is applied to accomplish his set goals which go far beyond normal human strength. When I returned to Berlin a few days ago, at one o'clock in the morning after two hard working days, I only wished to go to sleep. But no, I was requested to come to the Führer's apartment. He was still alert and working all alone. I gave him my report for the next two hours about the progress in the construction of the Reich's highways. All day from

The Führer on his 47th birthday.

principles and the flexibility needed for the extension of methods. The Führer is a stickler for principles and a dogmatist. He never shortchanges dogma and principle because he handles them with the superior flexibility of his technique and method. His goals never changed. The things he does today, he already wanted to do in 1919. The methods he used to reach his goals, were always changed, according to the situation.

In August, 1932, the Vice-Chancellorship was offered to him. With a few short words he declined. He had a feeling that the time was not yet right. The platform he was to be put on seemed too small to last. A bigger door to power was opened to him on January 30, 1933. Courageously he stepped across. He did not yet have the whole responsibility handed to him, but he knew it was a big enough base from which to start his fight for total control. The know-it-alls did not want to understand either. Today they have to humbly ask his forgiveness because he proved to be their superior, not only in tactics but also in strategic leadership of principles, which in their overbearing short-sightedness, they had claimed to defend.

The press published two pictures last summer, showing the Führer in heart-wrenching solitude. In the first he is greeting the passing Armed Forces from the window of the Reich's Chancellery. It was one day past June 30th on which he had had to wash away treason and mutiny with blood. His face was almost frozen from the cutting bitterness he had been living through during the past hours. In the second he is leaving the house of the president in Neudeck on his last visit to the dying General Field Marshal. His face is shadowed with pain and sadness over the mercilessness of death which will tear his fatherly friend away from him during the next few hours. On New Year's Eve 1934, he predicted with his prophetic eye to a small group of friends that there would be big dangers ahead and that we would most likely lose Hindenburg in the beginning of the new year. Now the inevitable had happened. You could read the pain of the nation in the stony face of a single person, not complaining but filled with sadness.

The whole nation looks up to him not only in adoration, but also with deep heartwarming love. The nation feels that it belongs to him and is one with him in body and spirit. That feeling is expressed in the smallest, most unimportant details of everyday life. In the Chancellery there rules a respectful camaraderie, which links the last SS man to the escort, with the Führer. On trips everybody stays in the same hotel and receives equal treatment. Therefore it is no wonder that especially the common people in his circle are the most faithful to him. They know instinctively that all this is far from a pose. It is the result of his natural inner nature, and a self-evident spiritual attitude.

morning till late at night he had handled great external, political problems, but still he had the energy to listen to my report, which had nothing to do with his current problems. Before the last Party day in Nuremberg, I was his guest for one week at Obersalzberg. Every night till six or seven in the morning, you could see the light burning in his window. The Führer dictated the big speeches he gave a few days later at the party convention. No law is passed in the cabinet unless that law was studied by him in the smallest detail. He is a specialist on all military questions. He knows as much about every piece of military equipment as his specialists. He has to know every detail when he gives them a lecture. His way of working is geared towards total clarity. Nothing is further away from him than nervous haste and hysterical eccentricity. He knows better than anybody that there are a hundred and more problems that have to be solved. He picks the two or three biggest problems, and does not let the smaller ones interfere with the solution of the big ones. He knows with certainty that once the big problems are solved, the second- and third-rate problems are almost taken care of by themselves.

In the solution of the problems he is proving the hardness necessary to fight one's way through

The Work Army, Reich's Party Day, 1935.

Bückeberg, 1934.

*Reich's President von Hindenburg and
Reich's Chancellor Hitler.*

*Heroes' Memorial Day, 1935.
In front of the Monument to Glory in Berlin.*

Reich's Party Day, 1935: the Work Soldiers.

A few weeks ago 50 young German girls came to his Chancellery asking permission to see him for a few moments. They are young Germans, born and living in foreign countries, who had spent one year in Germany's schools, and were now ready to return to their bleeding Homeland. He invited them all for dinner at his house. For hours they had to tell him about their small, moderate lives at home. While saying their goodbyes, they, with tears in their eyes, started to sing the song: "When Everybody Becomes Unfaithful." Between them stood the man who for them had become the essence of eternal Germany. He gave them friendly, comforting words to take with them on their hard road home.

He came from the people and so he remained. He who negotiates for two days in 15-hour meetings, with the statesmen of the world power, England, discussing the future of Europe, with his polished dialogue and masterly command of his arguments and numbers, speaks with the same obvious naturalness to the common people. He puts a wartime comrade at ease by using the familiar second person singular in speaking to him. The man who stands before him, his heart throbbing, may have thought for days about how to approach him and what to say to him. The smallest approach him with friendly trust, they feel he is their friend and protector. The whole nation loves him because they feel sheltered in his hands, like a child in his mother's arms. This man is fanatically possessed by his idea. For it, he sacrificed his happinesss and private life.

Only his work exists for him. Work is his fulfillment and he serves in inner humility as the most faithful worker of the Reich. An artist turns into a statesman. In his historical build-up, his true artistic talent is revealed. He does not need public tribute. His glory is his own everlasting accomplishment. We, who have the good fortune to be with him daily, receive only light from his light. We want to escort the train led by his flags and be his most obedient followers. Often in the circle of his oldest comrades-in-arms and closest confidantes, he said, 'It will be horrible when the first of us dies, and leaves an empty place that cannot be refilled.' A kind fate should leave his place occupied the longest, so the nation can continue for many decades under his leadership, on the way to new freedom, greatness and power. This is the honest and most impassioned wish that the whole German nation in gratitude is laying at his feet. And like us who are closely gathered around him, so the last man in the most remote town is saying at this hour:

'What he was, he is,
and what he is, he shall remain:
OUR HITLER.' "

Germany's strength.

The Führer and the Armed Services

BY LIEUTENANT COLONEL FOERTSCH

Adolf Hitler was a soldier in the German army. He volunteered wholeheartedly for the biggest war which any army ever fought. For four years he was bleeding in the front lines for his Fatherland, through the fury of raging World War battles, in dirt, mud and gas clouds. He was an attentive observer. He understood what the November Revolt never could have permitted to be understood, if they did not want their actions to be recognized as an unprecedented betrayal of the people: that a society is unable to function if it is unable to protect the world place of its lowliest son from seizure by enemies; that it cannot farm the land unless the sword gives security to the plow. He also saw what was missing in the old army, what sin was committed against them by the Reichstag during the liberal decade starting in 1914.

Like this, two basic goals showed themselves to him: First, restore the German right to maintain armed forces and at the same time create a new German army, strong enough to protect the German borders against attack. Second, build up the army through compulsory military service, according to the ideology that military service is an honorary tribute to the nation, therefore no unworthy person and no foreigner can join. At the same time, nobody will receive special privileges or preferred treatment.

The Führer saw with inner sympathy and great satisfaction that the Reich's Defense was able to keep the German army in shape, in spite of the pacifism and defeatism from the betrayal and the decay of the November Republic. Yes, in the scope of feasibilities they forged them into a strong and useful weapon. This was why an early alliance between the Führer and the Reich's Defense was formed, the National Socialist Party.

It was mostly the young officers who soon recognized that here stood a man who was capable on his own to raise up the German army once again. A few days after January 30, 1933, when the Führer had been elected the new Reich's Chancellor, he gathered all the high commanders of the army in the Reich's Ministry of the Army. He explained to them in detail the fundamental concepts of National Socialist politics. He assigned them their task and drew a clear-cut picture of what was expected of the armed forces (Wehrmacht) and what was their duty in National Socialist Germany. The public never was informed about this meeting. The time was not yet ripe to attract attention to these questions. Two years later the new German army was finally allowed to step into the daylight.

When Adolf Hitler wrote his work, MEIN KAMPF, he reminisced about the old German army, in which he had been for four years a simple soldier and later a lance-corporal. He remembered it with words, which express today and always the greatest pride of the German army:

"The army was the strongest school of the German nation, and not without good reason was the hate of all enemies directed against this protector of national self-preservation and freedom. You cannot give a more magnificent monument to this

Reich's Party Day, Nuremberg, 1935: the banners of the old army units.

Armed Forces Day, Nuremberg, 1935: Anti-aircraft gun.

Long distance defense.

Protection of the Coast.

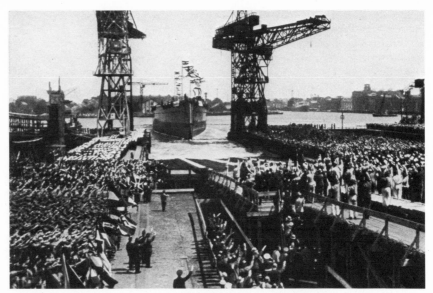

The christening of the pocket cruiser, "Admiral Graf Spee."

The Führer with his young sailors.

A visit to the fleet.

institution than the noteworthy truth that they are lied about, hated, fought against but also feared by all inferiors. What the German nation owes to its army can be expressed best in one word: 'EVERYTHING.' "

The army bred total responsibility at a time when this virtue was hard to find. It bred personal courage in a decade when cowardice threatened to turn into an epidemic. Self-sacrifice for the well-being of everybody was looked upon almost as stupidity and only those who knew how to put their own interest first were considered intelligent. This was the school that taught the individual German not to look for the salvation of the nation in the lying phrases of international fraternization, but in the strength and togetherness of their own people. The army called for strength of purpose during a time when the life of the people seemed to be guided by indecision and doubt.

It signified a decade in which the know-it-alls set the tone everywhere, holding high the basic ideal that one order is always better than none. This one basic ideal enclosed an unspoiled rugged health, which already would have been lost in our life if the army and its breeding had not seen to the renewal of this basic virtue. The army taught

Bombers over Nuremberg.

*German troops crossing the Rhine
at Mainz, March 7, 1936.*

that idealism and devotion be given to the Fatherland and its greatness. It bred a united nation in contrast to the separation of the classes, and had here perhaps as its only mistake the one year voluntary service.

The army held high a belief in quality in contrast to the Jewish democratic emphasis on quantity. Like this it also gave birth to the idea that what the newer times needed most was men. In the swamp of an overall growing softness and effeminacy, the army discharged every year 350,000 powerful young men. In two years of training they had lost the softness of youth and won steel-hard bodies. The young person who during this time practiced listening learned afterwards how to give orders. By his walk alone you could recognize the soldier.

This was the high school of the German nation. Not without reason fierce hate was concentrated on those who, because of envy and greed, needed and wished for the powerlessness of the Reich and the defenselessness of its citizens. What many Germans out of blindness or ill will did not want to see, the foreign world recognized. The German army was the most powerful weapon in the service of the freedom of the German nation and the

First planning of the Richthofen fleet.

in a position to accomplish this feat. When his decision of October 14, 1933, to turn his back on the League of Nations became known, the hearts of the soldiers, to the last one, throbbed with happiness for him because each one understood that with this, the rebuilding of the German free army had begun. It is no coincidence that, since that memorable day in Potsdam, the army marches along with the Storm Troopers and Party formations on all German holidays.

This new army portrays a true people's army in that birth, means or social position no longer make a difference just as the Party never, at any time, differentiated between people and belongs to the people. It belongs in the midst of them and therefore it does not consider it an order, but an inner foregone conclusion to celebrate the people's holidays with the people themselves. Whether it be the First of May or a day of thanksgiving, festivities or sad occasions or the great Party convention in Nuremberg, the army stands shoulder to shoulder with the people everywhere.

Thus, the Führer, in his great Reichstag speech on January 30, 1934, the anniversary of the National Socialist Revolution, was already able to tell them about the armed forces in these words:

Our new tanks.

feeling of its children. In one respect, the judgment of the Führer cannot be transferred from the old army to the new Wehrmacht because of the way it had to exist after the treaty in Versailles. Because it was not built according to the will of the people, its shape was forced on it from the outside. Not even two out of a thousand were allowed to serve in the army. The old Wehrmacht was denied the same extensive influence in the cultivation of the nation. That is why it was a matter of course for the Führer to replace this professional army with a true people's army. The soldiers also knew this and therefore it is not surprising that the decision of the Reich's President at that time, von Hindenburg, to give the Chancellorship to the Führer, was greeted especially in the army with enthusiasm. If it was at all possible for one power in Germany to free the army and navy from the tight shackles of Versailles, then it was the power of this Chancellor behind whom the strongest political movement of the Nation marched. It was obvious in the ranks of the old army that the act of deliverance would not be child's play, but that one could expect the greatest difficulties. Unwavering was the conviction that the Führer and only the Führer would be

The "Lützow" tower
and mast of
the "Admiral Scheer."

Our Luftwaffe.

*Reich's Party Day,
Nuremberg, 1935:
the Navy marching.*

*Armed Forces Day, 1935. The Führer
with his advisors; from left to right:
the Luftwaffe Chief Colonel General
Göring, the Army Chief General Field
Marshal von Blomberg, Colonel General
eral Baron von Futsch, the Navy
Chief Dr. Raeder.*

The "wind-dogs" of the Baltic Sea. A German speed boat.

"It is a unique, historical instance that between the force of the Revolution and the leaders of an extremely disciplined army, such heartwarming bonds appeared in the service of the people as between the National Socialist Party and me as their Führer on the one hand, and the officers and soldiers of the German army and navy on the other."

The armed forces and their leadership stood with unconditional loyalty and support behind the new state.

That the armed forces do not lead a separate existence but are National Socialist armed forces is, in a National Socialist state, an obvious fact. This is always expressed with proud joy in that everyone who serves, starting with the supreme commander down to the last recruit, carries the national emblem of the National Socialist movement on his uniform. Often the Führer stressed this fact and characterized the party and armed forces as the two pillars on which the construction of the National Socialist Third Reich was founded. With all severity he defined the Party as the political will carrier and the armed forces as the weapon carrier of the Nation. With awareness and out of innermost voluntary desire, the armed

forces became part of the National Socialist direction of the new state, and were linked with it for better or for worse. There is a direct connection between the introduction of the comradeship salute of the National Socialist Party into all celebrations of the party and the state and the introduction of the national emblem of the Movement into the armed forces just as there is at the Party convention, with the raising of the war-flag decorated with the swastika. The "Obligations of the German Soldier" are written in the National Socialist spirit, as expressed in the oath of allegiance; "I swear by God this holy oath, that I will give unconditional obedience to the leader of the German Reich and Nation. Adolf Hitler, the highest commander of the armed forces, and that I will be ready at any time, as a courageous soldier, to risk my life for this oath."

From the first day of his entering office, the Reich's War Minister did not leave any doubt that the National Socialist ideology had irrevocably to be the foundation of life in the German armed forces. In his speeches to the troops and on other occasions, he always called attention to and acknowledged the fact, that the pledge of loyalty to the Führer and his work, is honest and unim-

Visit to the fleet in Kiel.

peachable. The armed forces are deeply engrossed in the process of German rebirth. The Reich's War Minister himself formulated it once in an article in *Völkische Beobachter:* "The army came to the State as what she was, an inwardly clean, disciplined resource of power in the hands of her leadership. It serves this state and accepts it out of inner conviction. It acknowledges this leadership which gave it back its noblest privilege, not only to be the bearer of arms, but also bearer of unlimited trust acknowledged by the people and the state. Today the whole German Nation is penetrated by a soldierly spirit."

The strength which carries the armed forces along comes basically from the source of a strong faith in Germany and its right to life. Today the soldier stands deliberately in the midst of the political life of the people welded together in unity. Once again military service is an honored service to the German Nation. The armed forces have endured and passed the difficult test of discipline in Germany's darkest hour and sometimes under unspeakable stress.

The combat comradeship of the trenches in the World War, which Adolf Hitler made into the foundation of the new union of the people (Volks-

gemeinschaft), became the starting point of the great tradition the armed forces inherited from the old army. Closely involved with the whole nation stands the army which bears with pride the symbol of German rebirth in its steel helmet and uniform. It stands in discipline and loyalty behind the leadership of the state, the leader of the Reich, Adolf Hitler, who once came out of our ranks and will always remain one of us. Here is the real secret that binds the new army to the Führer. He is one of us.

It is the same secret that binds the Führer and the worker, the Führer and the political fighter, because they all can truly say: He is ours. The Führer came from a farm. He was a worker like millions and millions of his fellow Germans, and like millions of other Germans he lay in the trenches as a common soldier for four years of war for the existence of the homeland. He was a soldier, a brave soldier, who risked his life as a messenger in the middle of the hell of barrage. Today when World War veterans sit together with the Führer, they remember the time when their own risk of their lives for the Fatherland bound them together in great comradeship and they all know to whom they swear their personal oath, namely

"Aviso Grille", a new navy ship that the Führer wanted to visit.

the comrade of the great War and in his person, the legacy of all soldiers killed in action. This is what makes the armed forces mentally National Socialist: The Führer is their Führer. He will always remain a soldier, ready to defend himself with his own life against the enemy, and therefore he also has the right to ask for the lives of others. He recognizes the plights and sorrows of a soldier. He knows what he needs and what has to be kept from him. This he knows not from reports and stories, but out of his own great experience.

It is therefore clear that there is no greater pride today for the armed forces than to be linked with this man and when the troops parade before him, their eyes light up, their step becomes more regular and every muscle is tensed to the ultimate. The leadership knows that the new armed forces have this man alone to thank for their existence. He made it possible through tough, exhausting, detailed political work to resurrect German military sovereignty, and to restore the ancient right of the free German to join military service. The Führer always impresses upon young soldiers that this honorary duty, to be allowed to serve the people, also includes a huge obligation. Just as the armed forces have his total support in all that they need, so is his demand on them forceful. Every soldier is aware of the fact that it is the sacrifices of all the people that allow him to carry on this honorary duty.

After the wonderful military spectacle of the Party Day in 1935, in Nuremberg, the Führer had this to say to his soldiers; "If you have to make personal sacrifices to obedience and performance, subordination, hardness, endurance and efficiency, do not forget, my soldiers, that the whole German Nation also has made great sacrifices for you. We make these sacrifices with the conviction that it does not require a war to reward us for them. Truly you don't have to earn a title of glory for the German army—it possesses one already. You have only to preserve it. Germany has not lost its military honor, and least of all in the last war.

Make sure that the trust of the Nation will always be yours, just as it once belonged to the army whose glorious helmet you are wearing. Then the German Nation will love you, will believe in its army and sacrifice happily for it convinced that through it the peace of the Nation will be preserved and the rearing of the German people guaranteed. This is what the Nation wants, what it hopes and demands from you. And I know you will fulfill this demand, the hope and the desire, because you are the new German Reich's new soldiers."

In this way, the Führer and the armed forces and the people are one, just as the people and the Führer are one, bound not only by oath and promise, but also by the joint aspiration and will for a free and united, strong National Socialist Reich.

Aboard a warship, the Führer visits the Norwegian fjords.

Party Day of Freedom: The youngest drummers of the nation.

The Führer and the German Youth

BY BALDUR VON SCHIRACH

Our youth pays homage to the Führer in all parts of the Reich. Today Adolf Hitler belongs to an inflamed and captivated youth which rejoice over him and serve him. We have accustomed ourselves to it as a commonplace. Whether he drives during his travels through an uninterrupted lane of this youth or, during the great festive events of the Movement, at their parades and declarations, is surrounded by this youth like a wall, the youth is always where the Führer is; always and everywhere it declares itself for him.

This picture to which we Germans are so accustomed appears to the foreigner again and again as wonderful. The mythical conformity of the Na-

tion's leader with the young generation belongs to one of the mysteries that the foreigner calls "the German wonder."

Actually there is hardly a better expression to explain this complete unity among not only the classes, ethnic groups and denominations, but also among all the generations in our Nation. This appears to be a wonder even to us Germans: that the Führer could achieve directing all age groups in our Nation to one mutual ideal, which everyone in their own way tries to follow with their own characteristic strength. The young ones with the passion and the inspiration which always were the badge of the forward-rushing German youth;

the older ones with the quiet clearness, steadiness and ripe strength which distinguish their age group.

Thus Adolf Hitler bred a whole Nation to service an idea. The 10-year-olds are, with just as much awareness, carriers of his work and harbingers of his will as are the 30- and 40-year-olds. Yes, the younger ones feel especially strong bonds with the person of the Führer because they feel with the infallible certainty of their instinct that the Führer dedicated his thoughts and concerns especially toward them. They know he is serving the future which they themselves are.

Germany has, especially in the recent past, suffered infinitely under the opposition of the younger and older generations. Particularly in the decade following the great War, one could feel this conflict in almost all families. It is futile to make an inquiry as to whose fault it was. Only this much can be said about it: the lack of respect and discipline in the youth of that time was not alone a one-sided fault of the youth. This youth had no example to follow in the older generation. The so-called "statesmen" of that time could not inspire any enthusiasm with their personalities or work and because of that were rejected and despised.

After the Führer gave her his autograph, she had the luck to have her picture taken with him.

She recited her poems. The Führer on his election campaign in 1932.

The insufficient and false examples left were film- and sports-stars.

Should we reproach the youth of that time because it would not fulfill the expectations of its elders? Does not every teacher know that youth needs big and heroic models to develop in a way that is necessary for the Nation? Men whose heroic efforts in the World War should have inspired the youth were mocked and insulted by the press and, even worse, by important men in the government. And the heroic ideal could be publicly mocked without punishment as the height of stupidity.

In such circumstances it seems natural that the youth lost every motive and all moral backbone. Because the conduct of many members of the older generation was despicable, the youth drew the conclusion that all old people are despicable. Because cowardice was praised, they believed everybody good was cowardly and lost all feeling for right and wrong, restraints and law. The great sex trial of juveniles at that time as well as the overall juvenile delinquency during the years after the War, still live in our memories. They show us with terrifying clarity where even the German youth can fall if it doesn't have leadership.

We always see the Führer surrounded by children.
On the right, Baldur von Schirach.

Adolf Hitler attempted from the first day of his rule to lead the youth back to themselves. That this experiment succeeded to an extent which even the greatest optimists never expected is only thanks to his inexhaustible will power and persistence. Only too easily does the superficial observer overlook the combat years of the National Socialist Movement, the detailed work which had to be performed as prerequisite for the construction, the great slogans and battles of the Movement. The National Socialist Youth Movement, too, was not given to the Führer. Neither did it grow out of newspaper appeals and speeches alone, but as in every ground-breaking of the Movement, the Führer here has also year after year fought for the laws of the construction until he announced the fundamental thesis in accordance with which the youth leaders had to work.

When Adolf Hitler imprinted the words, "Youth must be led by Youth," a new stage in the educational history of the human race had begun. Only a genius can with one word close the past and at the same time open up the future. Adolf Hitler has with his slogan about youth education captured for his flag all the youth of his Nation. It is of no importance that the Führer's slogan was hardly understood at the beginning; yes, that people tried at first to scorn and ridicule it, like all program-controlled declarations of the Führer. It is also unessential that the Youth Movement, the construction of which was directed by this law, encompassed only a few thousand. Only one thing is important and essential: that Adolf Hitler out of the intelligence of this youth and with a sympathetic insight into peoples' natures, like no other statesman or teacher before him, could produce, organize and announce a thesis, which we felt even then had to build up, out of the small associations of that time, the largest Youth Movement in the world.

Aside from Adolf Hitler, all statesmen of the past and present looked upon the leadership of the youth exclusively from the viewpoint of the older generation and took it as an undifferentiated task. For them it was handed down, a matter-of-course, about which they no longer thought: the older ones take on the responsibility and management of the younger in their own circle. Big states' youth organizations in other countries are conceived and carried out in this way.

Adolf Hitler has, in contrast to all former educational methods, burdened the youth themselves with the responsibility for their actions. It was he who proclaimed responsibility is educational power. One of the most touching testimonies to the inner quality of the German youth is that they

Young Germany greets the Führer on his election campaign.

Children's hands.

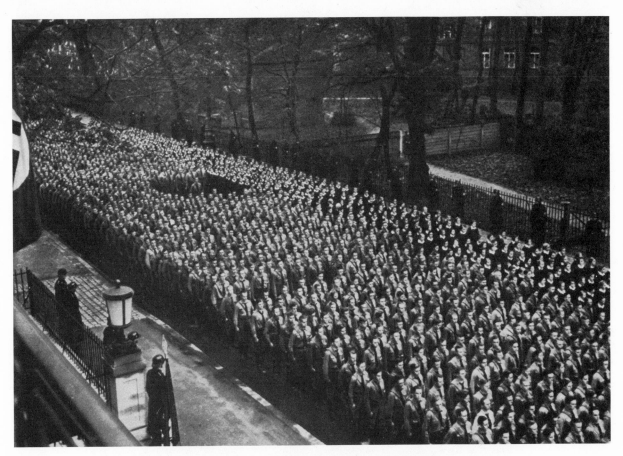

*Munich, November 9, 1935. Hitler Youth in front of the Brown House
before becoming full-fledged Party members.*

Hitler Youth as guests in Obersalzberg.

Power Party Day, 1934. In the stadium with the Youth.

did not disappoint the Führer's trust, but on the contrary, in spite of some differences and disorders, they strove to justify the trust, which they at all times perceived only as an honor and an obligation.

So the youth fell in line with the law of the Führer and by toilsome work, advancing step by step, has developed into a powerful community which has no equal in the world. All this without the pressure of a law, without the injunction of a minister, exclusively through the inner power of the idea which impels them. Can you imagine what it means that the Führer knew, even before

the takeover of power by National Socialism, that the majority of the German youth stood behind him? The Reich's Youth Day in Potsdam was held three months before the Führer became Reich's Chancellor and is still the largest youth assembly which the world has seen so far.

The Communist and Social Democrat youth organizations were already cut down before January 30, 1933, not through brute force, but through the mental conquest of their members by means of the National Socialist idea. That differentiates the Hitler Youth the most from youth organizations in other countries.

The Führer with the Youth at the Reich's Party Day, 1935.

They did not get their assignment later, but took part in the showdown for power. They have made sacrifices in this fight and in the spring of 1937 constituted voluntary groups that in the age groups of the 10- and 14-year-olds alone includes more than 90% of all juveniles.

Adolf Hitler pursues even today the work of his youth movement in all areas. Year after year he welcomes the winners of the Reich's professional competition in the Reich's Chancellery to congratulate them personally. He examines the architecture of the youth by viewing their demonstrations of the models of the youth hostels and their lay-

outs. In the course of this, he helps with advice and action taken from his own great experience in construction.

Often he himself establishes contact with the youth. When he meets a group of young people in Berchtesgaden or Berlin, he invites them and treats the surprised young people to coffee and cake. Then they sing their songs for him and he listens to the reports of their journey.

The birthday of the Führer is perhaps the strongest means of expression for this direct connection between him and his youth. You can see on the long tables in the Reich's Chancellery thousands of little presents which the boys and girls in the whole Reich thought give joy to their Führer: Handicrafts and handpainted postcards, embroidery and logbooks, all these things tell more than words how the thoughts of the young generation revolve around this man who presented our youth with an existence in freedom and with a sense of duty. How many times I could observe how the Führer seems to linger longer in front of these little and insignificant presents than in front of the expensive and sophisticated ones.

What seemed impossible a while ago and even as a demand seemed utopian became a convincing reality. In order to form this reality, this youth certainly had to make sacrifices. Some youth groups of the past, who honestly tried to reach a bigger goal, had to be abandoned in order to achieve the big union of all youth. And the Hitler Youth themselves had to lay out some dead comrades on the stretcher to arrive at this ultimate inner oneness and unity, without which no community on this earth can last. But the young killed in action died with the belief in the Führer and his coming Reich and the millions of young living are bound together by the same belief. They all feel themselves to be bearers of the obligation the Führer assigned to them and feel they are one with him in the service of the greatness of the Reich.

The work of Adolf Hitler can never vanish because all youth of the German Nation is joyful, ready to serve this endeavor for a lifetime, with responsibility and faithfulness, and finally surrender it to those who come after them. With such determination they greet the coming millennium.

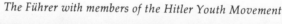

The Führer with members of the Hitler Youth Movement

The Movement's being honored at the Königsplatz in Munich, November 9, 1935.

The Führer and the National Socialist Movement

BY PHILIPP BOUHLER

An unknown soldier in the World War was temporarily blinded as a result of mustard gas poisoning on November 8, 1918, and confined to the military hospital in Pasewalk. Because of his reaction to the horrendous Stock Exchange uprising, he made the decision to become a politician and to take action himself in the destiny of his deluded and humiliated Nation. Nobody could have anticipated that this same man little more than 14 years later, as Führer and Reich's Chancellor would stand at the head of the entire German Nation.

Only Adolf Hitler himself, with the infallible confidence in the genius of his own power, knew the way to take. He also knew that even in chaotic postwar Germany, the political leadership would never fall to one individual, who only had his knowledge, his personality and the belief in himself to throw into the balance. He knew that the way to power in the State, which alone would allow for the possibility of changing the wretched situation in Germany, could only be achieved through a movement borne on by the idea of victory and fanatical belief that had to be tightly anchored and organized in its nucleus.

What would Frederick the Great be, without the tool, bequeathed to him by his royal father, without the army, with and through which he fought his victories? Adolf Hitler, too, created for himself the tool that was to give his politics a concrete foundation: He created the National Socialist Party. From the tiniest beginnings, he organically created his organization, based upon the idea of the leader (Führer) principle and voluntary followers. In his own party he broke first of all with parliamentary practices, placed fundamental responsibility at the top and put boundless authority on the bottom, in place of the democratic slogan that states the equality of all people and the rule of the majority.

125

The glorious monument to the Party members killed on November 9, 1923. Feldherrnhalle, Munich.

While German parliaments were bargaining for the personal advantage of individual cliques and exhausted themselves in fruitless ballots over the essential life problems of the German Nation; while under the eyes of the government, subversive elements trampled on honor and prestige, and wasted what remained of German national wealth; while the state stood by helplessly doing nothing; while the German Fatherland continued more hopelessly to stagger down into the gulf of political and economic slavery, Adolf Hitler forged the tool for the internal and external liberation of Germany. For 14 years he has navigated his Party through reefs, has in tough and untiring work

overcome all obstacles, until in spite of all setbacks, success after success came under his banner. Not because right was on his side (right can be bent). Not because blindly believing followers with holy fanaticism fought for victory (even the tremendous sacrifices of possessions and blood can be given in vain). Not because the opposition, driven by blind angry hate, made unforgivable mistakes in their will to annihilation. No, the Movement won because Adolf Hitler was its leader.

Because he is the Movement, because he in his person embodied the idea of National Socialism, today Germany is free. The Germany of disgrace

Reich's Party Day, 1934. The Standards.

and shame, which the Jews and deserters had made into the laughingstock of the world, exists no longer. Like a phantom, the years of external enslavement, inner disputes, the persecution and suppression of the German character inside our land, and an unparalleled corruption in all areas of public life, have vanished. The dream of the century has become a reality.

A self-reliant German Reich has come into being. Class hatred and snobbery have disappeared. There are no more parties in Germany. Fraternally united in striving towards one goal, the German tribes are obeying one command.

All this is the work of Adolf Hitler. And if he

had accomplished nothing else, he would have done this one thing. The German Nation, which lay defenseless on the ground for half a century, a plaything for its enemies, has once again won back its fitness for military service, and this would be enough to carve his name immortally on the Parthenon of history.

Remember what courage and faith, what limitless self-sacrifice and devotion became alive throughout the long years of the struggle in the beginning, with a small group of faithful followers that grew and grew, until it became a people's movement and finally an army of millions wearing a brown suit of honor. You may wonder why for

A repetition of the historic march on November 9, 1934.

Old party members in front of the Brown House in Munich, 1935.

Reich's Party Day, 1934

10 years and longer, thousands have joyfully and blindly obeyed him, putting their occupation and families behind him, suffering mockery and scorn, taking insults and giving their last pennies without asking for gratitude? Why have tens of thousands collapsed and hundreds gone to their deaths under the strokes of brutish adversaries with a last "Heil Hitler" on their pale lips? Why have mothers, from whom was taken their ultimate and most cherished possession, said: "I am proud of this sacrifice?"

When you ask yourself, how was it possible, to create from this tangled mass of parties one single strong Movement, above position and class differences and artificially nourished clan opposition, beyond all religious disputes and the most varied notions on the form of government, we always come back to the only answer: because Adolf Hitler was the leader of this Movement. The ingenious organizer, the fascinating speaker and master of propaganda, whom many an intellectual, sitting on his high horse, would have liked to disregard as the "Drummer," was always truly a born statesman. The hot-hearted daredevil who looked daringly into the face of danger and went forth to meet it. The man of circumspection, who knew how to wait, until the hour was ripe. The superior who saw through the tricks of his opponents and

Reich's Party Day, 1935.

who divided the wolves from the sheep. He has given this Movement created by him its ideological foundation, the quintessence of his political and philosophical realizations, born in the hard apprenticeship and suffering years of his youth, and purified and hardened in the fire of the World War. He was and is the dynamic force who nourishes and drives the Movement forward.

You cannot characterize this unique bond between the Movement and the Führer more touchingly than Rudolf Hess, when in opening the Reich's Party Congress convention in 1933 in Nuremberg, the congress of victory, he said, "My Führer, you were for us as leader of the Party the guarantor of victory. When others advised us to compromise, you remained uncompromising. When others let their courage sink, you spread new courage. When others left us, you took hold of the flag more determinedly than ever."

Adolf Hitler never cared about his own person. For example, when on November 9th, with ultimate determination, he marched from the Bürgerbräukeller, at the head of the column, which broke down under a shower of bullets in front of the Feldherrnhalle or when on the fatal morning in Wiessee, accompanied by only a few faithful followers, with his own hand he arrested the traitors.

The whole history of the Party then is a single example of the unheard-of personal commitment and boundless devotion of the Führer to his work. For him it gave no rest, no holidays. A 14- or even 16-hour day was no rarity for him. Through long nights he would dictate, design proclamations, leaflets and posters in his car, train or airplane. Adolf Hitler's special oratorical performance in holding up to four giant assemblies on one day in

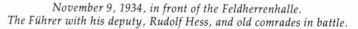

November 9, 1934, in front of the Feldherrenhalle.
The Führer with his deputy, Rudolf Hess, and old comrades in battle.

different big cities is not surpassed in judgment. There is no town, no city that does not have a place in his memory. Menacing crowds of misled fellow Germans following his car with muffled muttering or with wild screaming, or even with stone throwing . . . closely packed mobs of people, testify their love for him by roaring "Heils" and by a rain of flowers . . . overflowing town bars, in which a couple of hundred, and crowded city halls, in which tens of thousands, contributed frenzied applause to his words . . . the blond children of believing mothers are lifted into his car . . . or the modest lamp at an airport that sparkled like a star, saving him from going off the runway.

When the decision had been made and the election campaign completed, then the Führer sat all night with his faithful followers near the loudspeaker, waiting for the results. With throbbing heart and with bated breath they listened to the individual announcements. They wrote the results down, calculated, totaled and when the cautious estimated figures were reached, and when even the most daring expectations were surpassed, then the jubilation had no bounds.

There were also days of failures and setbacks. The Führer never despaired. He never let his spirit sink. After unprecedented successes, he issued the slogan, "The fight continues immediately," and worked with renewed vigor when the set goal had not been achieved.

When in the November Elections 1933, a recession of National Socialist voices was noted, compared to the past election, Adolf Hitler threw himself at the same hour—it was way past midnight—with grim energy into preparations for the next battle. He thought of ways and means to increase

Fifteen Years' Festival of the oldest group of National Socialist members in Rosenheim, 1935.

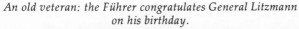

An old veteran: the Führer congratulates General Litzmann on his birthday.

Party Day of Freedom. The Führer is waiting for the columns of Brown Shirts.

the already powerful propaganda work of the party into gigantic proportions in order to lessen the gap next time.

Sometimes it seemed like the physical and mental tension of Adolf Hitler would go beyond the realm of the possible. Once, after an exhausting night drive from Berchtesgaden, he arrived in the early morning hours at his hotel in Bayreuth. At once he received telephone news of the crisis that had arisen in Berlin on account of the mutiny of Storm Trooper Leader Stennes, and which had taken on a threatening mien. Instantly back into the car and on with a dashing drive to Berlin. There there were conferences and negotiations

until evening, and subsequently speeches to the Storm Troopers in all storm localities. The same night back to Munich. Immediately into the Brown House. From there the revolt was finally crushed. Impromptu dictation for hours, from shorthand to typewriter, special publications, summonses, leaflets, conferences, all that again into the sinking night. And again, an attempt to split the Movement was smashed.

The ceaseless work for the well-being of the Movement, the everlasting concern for its fate, have accompanied Adolf Hitler all through the long years of the fight. In this work, the constant fight, against misery and privations and against

The blood-flag of 1923 at the Reich's Party Day in Nuremberg.

the tormenting sorrows, he grew to the mighty stature in which he stands today before Germany and the world.

Whoever experienced the Führer in times of extreme trouble, on days on which the very existence of his Movement was in doubt, knows that he is at his best when lightning-like actions are required. He also knows that for this man there exists no protective boundaries but that the hour of danger will see him, in the past as well as in the present and future, at the focal point of events, at the head of his followers. Whoever saw the Führer at such moments knows that this man, with eyes of unlimited kindness, turns hard and pitiless when his work is touched or danger threatens his Movement.

Adolf Hitler is generous like no other man. He, who has restored the right to personality in Germany, does not want lackeys. He wants to be surrounded by honest men who are used to thinking and acting independently, ready to take on responsibility. He can tolerate a frank word, and his superior insight is always accessible to the compelling logic of a convincing reason. Because he can not use creatures as tools, he wants to raise up personalities. Therefore, he gives his staff members the greatest freedom of action. Every petty limitation and constriction on the work of other

Admiral Raeder with the German Fleet.

people is foreign to him. He draws the outlines, he shows the direction, but he leaves everybody enough latitude. He measures by character and achievement, not by the details of How? Where? When? and not by protocol, which is distasteful to his soul. He is always ready to forgive a mistake. He looks the other way when somebody misses the mark or uses wrong methods. He often overlooks, with gigantic patience and indulgence, personal defects and inadequacies which constitute part of the human character.

But woe to anybody who tries to shake the foundation of the Movement. Woe to anybody who dares to sin against the spirit of the Movement and tries to destroy the character of its organization. Woe to anybody who pledged to be loyal to the Führer and Movement and commits a breach of faith. For him there is no pardon. In his case nothing helps. Here no rank or name counts. Here even the merits, no matter how great, are not weighty enough; his scale tips and he falls back into the Nothing from which he came. Like the wanderer who laboriously climbs to the top of the hill looks back on the path which twists over heights and through lowlands to the top, Adolf Hitler can look back today, as the Führer of Germany, onto his path which led him after a four-

teen-year struggle to the top of the Nation. In a matchless ascent, overflowing with dangers, sacrifices and hardship, but also overflowing with belief, happiness and proud, inner satisfaction.

Adolf Hitler looks back often and gladly. Because he possesses a rich measure of what was always the mark of a truly great human: gratitude. Thankfulness towards Providence whose work sometimes seemed mysterious, till fate showed the only right way. Thankfulness towards his Movement and towards his old comrades-in-arms, who stayed faithful to him in good and bad days. He knows them all personally; he shakes their hands with honest joy when he meets them unexpectedly anywhere in the country, and they can always be sure of his concerned sympathy. Especially with his old Storm Troopers and SS men, he is united in a warm comradeship. The soldierly nature in him has always found the right words for the combat troops of the party, which was created out of the military spirit.

A combat movement was what the National Socialist Party was, from the real beginning, and therefore like a magnet it drew the natural fighters. In the early days of the Movement, when the Storm Troopers developed slowly out of the organizer troops of the party (which, in turn, was created out of a handful of war comrades of the Führer) you could see Adolf Hitler in the middle of the soldiers. He demonstrated with them in the streets; with them he visited the assemblies of his opponents, into which is interruptions scored like direct hits. During parades away from home, he shared the layer of straw in mass accomodations with them. When the red mob attacked the demonstration lines of the Storm Troopers, he stood fast in the thickest turmoil. He himself dealt powerful blows.

It is the power of his personality that captivates the people and never lets them go. His personality is the fountain from which the fearful draw courage and the despairing draw new hope. As Adolf Hitler gives his Movement new encouragement and strength, his spirit and his blood flowing through the giant organism of the party, so in return is his Movement a fountain of strength to him. It is his home. It is the ground which holds his roots. Just as the National Socialist Movement cannot be thought of without Adolf Hitler, the Führer can not be thought of without this Movement.

Besides, with this Movement he created the means to take the helm of German fate and step by step to convert his ideas into reality. The Movement and the pursuit are so much a part of him that he could not live without them.

The burden of business takes up most of the time of Adolf Hitler, the statesman, but even today he takes an active part in all events inside the organization and keeps in close touch with the leading men of the party. Whenever a Reich's or District Leader, a high leader of the Storm Troopers, SS or of a Youth Organization comes to Berlin, he is a guest of the Führer in the Reich's Chancellery.

No wonder that even today, as the Chancellor of the German people, he feels happy among them. Often he is a witness to the marriage of an old fighter or makes a party member happy by becoming godfather to his son. Often he entertains Storm Trooper-comrades in his own house or receives them in the Reich's Chancellery. Often he visits their modest memorial celebrations in the traditional restaurants or in the casino of the Brown House. When he is surrounded by smiling faces of young and old men in brown shirts, then, as before, Adolf Hitler is one of them, comrade among comrades.

This human side of him is the picture of the

Hitler with Storm Trooper youth in the Brown House in Munich.

Visit to Landsberg Fortress.

Führer which millions carry in their hearts. The people can be forced to obedience. The respect, earned through a great accomplishment, they give freely and gladly to the man at their head. But the love and adoration which the Führer receives could not be attained by force by any power in the world. They have their roots in the personality of Adolf Hitler.

When he is tired and run-down, the contact with the Movement revives him. When he speaks in front of National Socialist Assemblies and looks into the believing eyes of thousands who are eagerly looking up to him, then the electrifying spark which jumped from him to the masses

jumps back to him and gives him new energy and thirst for action. This constant living flow between Führer and follower is the last secret of Adolf Hitler's success and of the success of the National Socialist Movement. This fateful linking of Führer and Movement, this mutual community for better or for worse, is the reason why Adolf Hitler feels pulled back by magic strength to the historic towns of the Movement, to all the familiar places for which he has lasting memories.

Sometimes he thinks with nostalgia about the past when it was hard to be a National Socialist. The small, dark room in an old house in the Sterneckergässchen in Munich which used to be

Reich's Party Day, 1935. Standard-bearers and mourners.

the party headquarters in the early days of the Movement was kept in its original condition, according to the wish of the Führer, after he took power, to remind people in the future of the beginning. After Adolf Hitler had become the German Reich's Chancellor he revisited the little room and was greeted by the same big red posters on the walls which he had designed to call the population of Munich to the assemblies of the National Socialist Party. The same great red posters which announced the first breach with people poisoned by Marxism and which slowly drew larger and larger crowds in front of the advertising kiosks in Munich until the signs were banned by police for

traffic reasons. He found the first leaflets he had written in which he pitilessly settled with the adversaries of the German nation. He held in his hand a cigarette case which used to hold petty cash. Old pictures came to life and passed through his memory.

In this room, which hardly ever sees the daylight, he had fought hard to convince the advisory committee of the young party that the Movement needed the support of the labor movement for the fight against Marxism, and that to accomplish this purpose it should use propaganda. Finally his insight won and Adolf Hitler's popularity grew since the success of his ideas was no longer deni-

The exhibition of National Socialist Formations in the Munich Konigsplatz, November 9, 1935.

Motorized Storm Troopers before the Führer, Reich's Party Day, 1935.

A picture from the Landsberg Fortress, 1924.

The Führer's visit ten years later to his cell.

Political battleground. An orator speaks and the Führer makes short notes.
From left to right: Hess, Rust, the Führer, Zörner, Kerrl.

*The Führer among his closest collaborators on the eve of
the Reichstag's election of March 29, 1936.*

able. The young party was saved from the fate of being forgotten as an insignificant club. It turned into a Movement which filled more and more people with his concept until it gave Germany a different aspect because now it had a leader.

November 9, 1933 marked the 10th anniversary of the day on which Adolf Hitler made the desperate attempt to change Germany's fate. Honorless, defenseless, our Fatherland stood against a world full of enemies; internally torn, powerless and lacking united will-power, at the mercy of a group of mutineers eager for plunder. The insanity of inflation drove unchecked towards disaster. Like hyenas, the separatists crept around the land and waited for the right moment to destroy the German Reich once and for all. Now or never was the time for action.

Adolf Hitler took action. The attempt was a failure, the revolt collapsed. Not only because traitors covered themselves with disgrace.

Now, 10 years later, the Führer recognizes in this blow of fate the work of a kind Providence. Would the Movement, which was not ready at the time, have been able to accomplish the task if the revolt had succeeded? The German people were not enough taken by the National Socialist idea to complete a total mental change after the political takeover. And that was necessary to replace the old system with the new philosophy of life. Idealism alone cannot build a state. The time was not yet ripe. The Movement did not have all the prerequisites for the takeover of power.

But they had to march in Munich on November 9th. In spite of it the first in-blood-witnesses to the Movement had to give their young lives in

front of the Feldherrnhalle. Their blood was the semen for the new age in the German nation. It was a moving ceremony which on this fateful day of the Movement and the whole German nation held all of Munich captivated.

On the evening before the revolt, the old fighters met in the historic assembly room at the Bürgerbräukeller. From there the uprising began. Here the Führer with his raiders entered the meeting of the United Patriotic Association of Bavaria, during the speech of Commissioner von Kahr, and announced the National Revolution. Here you can still see the mark of the pistol shot he fired at the ceiling to give the signal. Here Kahr, Lassow and Seisser gave their word to support the new National administration, though a few hours later they broke their pledge.

The Führer looked back on those great moments and then reminisced about the following years which, through continued struggle, led to victory.

For a long time Adolf Hitler sat with his followers and exchanged words, greetings or looks with everybody. On the next morning he once again collected his fighters around himself. They lined up as they had ten years earlier. They all were dressed in the plain brown shirts. As then, they met at Ludwig's Bridge and marched through the decorated street of the town of the Feldherrnhalle. On the Odeonsplatz stood the immense brown and black lines of the Storm Troopers and SS surrounded by packed masses. In front of them were their standards. It was an unforgettable moment when the parade came close. The Führer himself, deeply moved, spoke touching words in remembrance of the first in-blood-witnesses to the Ger-

The Führer in Nuremberg. Reich's Party Day, 1935.

man revolution. He slowly walked down the steps of the Feldherrnhalle to the front of the new monument he unveiled. It was heart-rending when he put down the large wreath on the marble slab with the greeting to the dead comrades, "You have won." Since that ceremonious hour, two honor guards of the SS stand at both sides of the monument, and all passers-by respectfully raise an arm in the German greeting. According to the wish of the Führer, this day will be glorified now and in all the future years.

About a visit in the Landsberg Fortress—ten years after he was a prisoner there for one year

with his faithful followers—one of his oldest fighting companions and constant escort, SS brigade leader Julius Schaub, says the following:

"After the truly heroic fight and the victorious breakthrough of the National Revolution, the Führer wanted to visit Landsberg prison, in which he had been imprisoned for over a year and in which he wrote the major portion of his book MEIN KAMPF. On the afternoon of October 7, 1934, a sunny, clear autumn day, the Führer, SS Colonel and Munich Counsellor Maurice and I, drove to Landsberg. The three of us had spent our days together in the fortress-prison. The autumn wind

The Führer holding the Party standard at the Party Day of Freedom.

played with the leaves on our way over Pasing, past the Ammersee and into Bavarian Swabia. Shortly before Landsberg we stopped for a moment in a glade. The escort cars were sent on ahead to inform the prison about the impromptu visit of the Führer and to make it possible to enter the fortress without creating a fuss.

During the drive the memories of those early days in Landsberg came back to us. And the closer we came, all the more alive seemed the pictures and episodes which had been our existence ten years ago as prisoners at Landsberg. Names like Hess, Kriebel, Weber, Kallenbach, Fischer, Froeschl and more were mentioned. We spoke about 'Mufti,' the name we had given to the senior government counselor who was in charge of our welfare.

From a distance we could see the gates and walls of the beautiful little town and the Führer told us the story of his release from prison a few days before Christmas, 1924, how Adolf Mueller picked him up in a old Benz and took a picture of him standing next to the car in front of this very gate. Through the gate we entered the town, and drove through narrow streets to the splendid marketplace. Our visit was such a surprise that only a

few people in the streets recognized the Führer. The drive went on through town and over the Lech Bridge.

Then the roofs of the prison came into view on our right. It looked like a little fortress built in the conventional star-shape. A small street, passing development houses, led to the entrance of the prison.

Wives and children of prison officials quickly lined up on the street with bouquets of flowers after they received news of the Führer's visit. The Führer left the car and stepped under the huge front gate through which he had entered the fortress for the first time on November 11, 1923. The prison officials were deeply touched by this meeting. Some of them had worked there at the time of the Führer's imprisonment.

The bunches of keys rattled. It was the same tune as before, when, in the monotony of prison, time crawled into the tight cells. Then the order: Go to sleep. Doors were locked and the steps of the guard sounded further and further away.

Slowly the Führer, with me and Maurice at his side, retraced the way which he had walked hundreds of times 10 years ago, and on which many of his thoughts came to him, thoughts

142

which have taken shape and become a reality today. Around the prison chapel, past a blockhouse which 10 years ago had been occupied by men of Hitler's Strike-force.

Behind this blockhouse connected by a two-story building is the cell block. When we turned at the corner, the Führer stopped involuntarily for a moment. One of the windows above belongs to cell 7, which had been his home for one year. A passing guard unlocked the small door which leads into the floor of the building containing the cells. Flowers had been put on the tables and garlands around the doors. This part of the prison is no longer in use but is kept as a historic monument, the external sign that the spirit cannot be subdued with chains. The men who were supposed to be destroyed in prison found on the contrary strength in it to start the fight again and bring it to a victorious end.

A small staircase leads to the first floor, in which the Führer, Rudolf Hess, lieutenant colonel Kriebel and the Oberland leader Dr. Weber, had been kept. All the doors open into the corridor. Above cell number 7 a plate reminds us of the Führer's prison time.

On the tabletop was a guest book in which the Führer signed his name, now ten years after he had left Landsberg. He stepped to the window through which he had so often looked, past the walls into the country and Heinrich Hoffman took a picture of him to capture this historic visit. The Führer showed us a picture which had been taken of him on the same spot 10 years earlier.

Then the Führer looked at the block with the visitor's room where old fighting comrades had visited him often ten years ago. They kept the organization going for him and that was his support after he left prison.

The sun started to set when the Führer stepped out into the courtyard. Everything was the same as before. Out of filial love nothing had been changed. Next to the wall runs a small path, which was named Adolf Hitler Path. When the other inmates passed their time with games, the Führer walked this path, deep in thought, or speaking with a comrade.

Darkness started to fall as we reached the gate again. The Führer spoke a heartwarming farewell to the old officials, who still could not believe that the man whom they used to guard as prisoner stood now before them as the Führer of the Reich.

Meanwhile the news of the Führer's visit traveled from mouth to mouth in Landsberg. When we returned, the town was overflowing with people who wanted to get a glimpse of the Führer. Only slowly could the car proceed through the joyful people. Shoulder to shoulder they stood in the market place and in the narrow streets, all the way to the gate. What a meeting this was.

Ten years ago we prisoners published secretly a satirical newspaper called *The Landsberger Honorary Citizen*. Today, ten years later, this title is reality. Once forced to be a citizen, Adolf Hitler is today an honorary citizen of the town of Landsberg and the whole population of the town cheers for him. Up at the gate where he once stood on a cold gray winter's day next to Adolf Mueller's car to have his historic picture taken—the one which shows the Führer at the beginning of a new life— we stopped again. Henrich Hoffmann took a picture.

Night had fallen and we drove back to Munich. We were quiet in the car. Everybody was filled with the events of the last ten years and the big changes they had brought. Many things born in solitude had become realities. Over the fortress walls the German Nation had received from its Führer the most precious gift: Freedom."

A special interest of the Führer was always the Reich's Party Days of the National Socialist Party. They were the visible expressions of the size and unity of the Movement. They were the days of great military reviews, to which the Brown-shirted fighters came from all parts of Germany. They were and are the milestones, on which you can follow the development and growth of the Movement. The first Party Day in Munich in January, 1923, was still a local event, but the next three-and-a-half years later in Weimar showed Germany and the world that the Movement was not dead, it was alive and fighting with all its might for a comeback. After the Party Days of 1927 and 1929 in Nuremberg, Adolf Hitler declared this old town the site for all future Party Days.

It is characteristic of the will of the Führer that he always tried to give his Movement its own traditions. The preparations for each individual Party Day was always an inner need for the Führer. During the time of the struggle, he himself often went deep into debt in order to raise funds to enable as many Storm Troopers as possible to participate. He himself outlined the program to the smallest detail. He made the guidelines for the different special sessions in which lectures and discussions about special questions, like youth, women, students and overall political views, etc., were held. He personally supervised the great preparatory work which included transportation, accommodations and food supplies for the masses. The organization of special trains, the preparation of mass lodgings, the planning for mass food supplies, and later the setting up of a field kitchen were all questions whose importance grew to gigantic proportions with the expansion of the Reich's Party Days. Countless times the Führer went with his staff to Nuremberg to check on the forthcoming preparations until the curtain rose and the play began before the eyes of the inspired masses. It always had the same basic framework, but each time brought new impres-

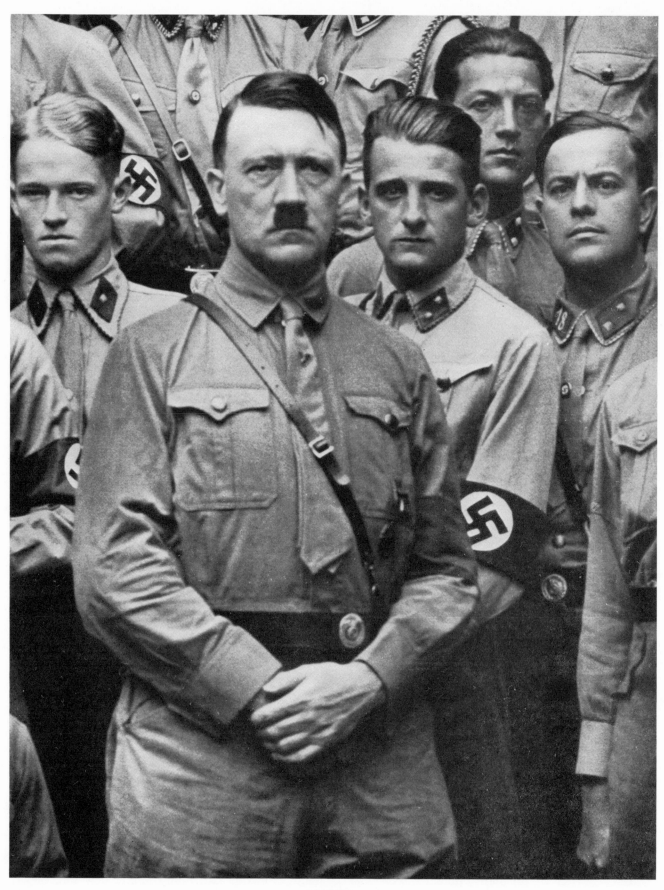

Adolf Hitler
with members of the Führer-School.

sions of unsurpassed beauty and power. That the Führer included in the great number of honorary guests also some of his oldest party comrades and the bereaved of dead fighters, was a natural honor he felt bound to do. It was after the victorious revolution that the Führer could make the necessary preparations to celebrate the Party Day exactly according to his will. The first changes were made on the big square in Luitpoldhain, which was picked for the parade of the SS, Storm Troopers and the presentation of the colors. The giant grandstand was built and was towered over by a giant eagle in the old Zeppelinfeld where, since 1933, the big parades of the political leaders are held.

The most powerful future project of the Führer, on which construction has now started and which will take eight years to complete, will be the cultural monument of the National Socialist Movement. With its gigantic dimensions it will testify to the omnipotence of the idea embodied in these proud buildings for future generations to admire.

On party property in the southeast part of Nuremberg a city is growing; independently from the city of Nuremberg, it has its own water and utility plants and also its own canal system. On the great camp-site a tent town will be erected that can accomodate up to 500,000 people. The Congress Hall, whose foundation-stone will be laid during the next few days, can hold 65,000 people. For armed forces parades a special field is being built which has room for 400,000 spectators. Broad roads and a train station will provide for easy access. At last an 80–90-meter-wide roadway, for the review march, has been built. A special administrations union was established which included representatives of the Party and the State, the German National Railway and the town of Nuremberg. This was to assure a uniform execution of this enormous task. When this task, whose progress the Führer follows with joyful pride and inner sympathy, is completed, then the Reich's Party Day will be even a greater concentration point for the show of strength of Nationalist Socialist Germany and therewith in truth the Reich's Day of the German Nation.

Years ago the Führer made the comment: "Soon I have to go to Berlin, because Berlin is the center of the Political Life. But the heart of the Movement will always remain in Munich." He has kept to his task. Near the Brown House, which has been for years for the world the outstanding symbol of National Socialism and near the other buildings which are housed by sections of the leadership of the Reich, two gigantic buildings are being built: the Führer Building and the Administration Building. They are the plastic expression of the Führer's will. He has an apartment in Munich as before, and whenever he can he returns to this second home of his. During his visits he never misses a chance to re-visit the Brown House, the place of his Work. There the conferences of the Leaders of the Reich were held, as well as all important debates of the party. The Führer gave Munich the official title "Movement City," to immortalize the unity of the Party with this town. With this present, he gave Munich his thanks for the first successes which it gave to his political work, for the sacrifices which it brought to the Movement and for the faithfulness to him which it always maintained. This is the birthplace of the Movement. Here the Movement had first to prove itself. Here were the early meetings, at first small and modest but later increasingly turning into mass meetings. Here started the first parliamentary fights, and the first punches fell in the disputes with the Marxist parties. The floor in the Feldherrnhalle is blessed with the blood of the first martyr for the National Socialist idea. Here the big trial was held which brought the name of Adolf Hitler into the world for the first time. From here it started its victorious march through the whole of Germany.

Adolf Hitler never was a party leader in the normal sense, just as the Nationalist Socialist Party was never a party like any other. The Party was only the organizational nucleus of the larger National Socialist Movement, which today is the only political carrier of the will of the German Nation. From the beginning, its purpose was to absorb the many other parties in Germany and thereby do away with all other parties in Germany, replacing them with people's unions. The National Socialist Party was never for Adolf Hitler's own aggrandizement. From the start he only saw in it the active nucleus of the German People, and beyond that the aim of his desire, for which he fought, worked and worried—

"Germany, nothing but Germany."